AF437138

DIRECT YOUR LiFE

DiRECT YOUR LiFE

OR SOMEONE ELSE WILL

STOP THE RERUNS, TAKE BACK CONTROL, AND
MAKE YOUR LIFE BETTER THAN ANY MOVIE

TONY SURiANO

For permissions requests, speaking inquiries, and bulk order options,
contact: contact@tonysuriano.com

Published in the United States by:
Suriano Books
Cincinnati, Ohio
www.tonysuriano.com

Cover Design and illustrations: Tony Suriano
Layout & Formatting: SelfPublishing.com
Author Photo: Mikki Schaffner

Names: Suriano, Tony, author.
Title: Direct Your Life or Someone Else Will: Stop the Reruns, Take Back Control, and Make Your Life Better Than Any Movie / Tony Suriano.
Description: Cincinnati, Ohio: Tony Suriano, 2026.
Library of Congress Control Number: 2026903401
Subjects: LCSH: Self-actualization (Psychology) | Success—Psychological aspects.
BISAC: SELF-HELP, Personal Growth, Success

ISBN: 979-8-90057-145-4 (paperback)
ISBN: 979-8-90057-144-7 (ebook)

First Edition, April 2026
Printed in the United States of America.

If you're reading this copyright page right now, stop.
Time is precious—and so are you.
Turn the page and start directing your life.

This book is dedicated to YOU—the reader who's ready to step into the role of the Director and live on your terms... so you don't reach the end filled with regret.

I know it's hard to stay on course, but practice makes progress.

Too many people have died with their magic still locked inside. It doesn't have to be you.

And in truth, to my past self, who fell into false dichotomies that disempowered him, drew dark conclusions about humanity, grew bitter from feeling misunderstood, and chose to close off instead of taking action.

The negative nihilist.

You nearly gave up...

But you didn't.

You stayed alive long enough to turn the story around and take on your hero's journey. You stepped into the Director's chair.

Thank you.

CONTENTS

ACT I
WRITE YOUR STORY

ACT II
BUILD YOUR CAST & CREW

THE DiRECTOR'S MANIFESTO

Directing your life is simple—but not easy.

It's not about controlling everything or everyone.

It's like the Serenity Prayer: change what you can, accept what you can't, and continually gather the wisdom to know the difference.

Outstanding Directors show up as their best selves.

They follow their heart.

They stay present with people.
They admit when they're wrong.

They live in joy, rain or shine.
They risk rejection, embarrassment, ostracism—even hatred—for a meaningful pursuit.

When you stop drifting and start directing, you'll know it.

When you're drifting, you look up one day and can't figure out how you ever got so far away...

Far away from that relationship, your health, your career—and most often, yourself.

Someone else was directing.

But your life is *your* life, and it's meant to be full of connection, laughter, growth, and meaning.

Better than any movie.

It starts with hyper-awareness sustained by relentless drive and dark humor: the kind of magic that feeds your soul and everyone around you.

Here's how it becomes real:

There's a proven system that can lead you through your own hero's journey so you can consistently direct your life.

If you want to stop the reruns, take back control of what you can, and let go of what you can't. It's simple, not easy, but *always worth it.*

And it's my absolute pleasure to share what I've learned—*and what I'm still learning*—as you discover how to direct your own life.

Take a seat in the Director's chair.

This is where you belong.

DI·RECT·OR   /də-ˈrek-tər/ · noun

Someone who refuses to drift.
They take responsibility for their story—scene by scene, choice by choice.

They pay attention, lead with intention, and act before they feel ready.
They fall, recalibrate, rise again, and find humor in the entire sequence.

They use discomfort as fuel and pursue meaning over approval.

They don't wait for permission. They create momentum.
They don't audition for their own life. They direct it.

And in doing so, they bring the magic—not just for themselves, but for everyone around them.

BEFORE YOU DECIDE

"Until you make the unconscious conscious, it will direct your life and you'll call it fate."

—Carl Jung

I was balancing on a thirteen-foot wall along the Los Angeles freeway at night—stealing and hiding in the shadows.

I didn't do drugs or alcohol.
But I was always trying to get away with something.

I became a thief, habitually stealing with my delinquent friends—not because I needed the money, but for the temporary hit of significance and dopamine.

Then I'd give most of it away, because I didn't believe I deserved to receive anything. Even on my birthdays, I'd refuse gifts.

That's how twisted my logic and emotions were. I was like Robin Hood with a self-loathing complex.

My character was drifting.

Then one night, I found myself stealing again.
This time, I was alone.
I felt disconnected. Hollow.

I was wasting my time and my life.

That was the night I finally admitted the truth.
The life I was living wasn't a story. It was an unfulfilling loop.

I couldn't keep living this way.

Not everyone has to hit rock bottom to make a life-changing commitment. But everyone has to stop and decide.

That was the night I understood something I couldn't unsee. Your life is always being directed.

The only question is—will you be the Director... Or will someone else?

THE BLANK PAGE

Most mornings, life feels like staring at a blank page.

You know the one. A vast, empty space that's supposed to hold your masterpiece, but instead, it mocks you with its nothingness.

For a fleeting moment, you might think, *"Ah, peace."* But more often, it's panic: *"I don't know what I'm doing. Where am I going? Who am I? Get me the hell outta here and to the café—iced matcha tea, macadamia milk, cinnamon on top, no sugar please!"*

What? You don't order that?

But that blank page is where your freedom begins.

After that matcha, I decide to face that page with a naked heart. Because I know this:

The blank page is an adventure. It's where you create your vision, break through your barriers, and find your magic.

It's where you direct your life.

WHAT'S MY MOTIVATION?

Twenty years ago, I wrestled with a strong butterfly feeling about writing a book.

The thought looped like this:

If I write a book, that must mean I've made it. It would give me credibility. A legacy.

Then the doubt kicked in:

You're too young.
Who are you to offer wisdom?
You have to be successful first.

But another voice kept pushing back.

If I do the work, study deeply, and pour everything I have into it...maybe I could create something that actually changes lives.

Instead, I spent several decades directing and writing over 80 film projects: narratives, commercials, experimental pieces, and music videos.

Along the way, I became obsessed.

Not just with filmmaking, but with understanding people—
how we communicate,
why we self-sabotage,
what really drives us,
and why we keep hiding our purpose without realizing it.

And the more I learned, the clearer my crusade became:

To create content that brings that purpose back into view so you can feel magic every single day...
and start living a life better than any movie.

I know that might sound like a lofty dream. But dreams are the previews for the film called Your Life.

This book demanded the most focus I've ever poured into *anything*. And every time *resistance* showed up, I had to tap into the wisest strategy I know—pick up the baseball bat and swing every day.

That's how this got finished.
That's how it got to you.

It exists to guide you out of drifting, steer you away from the traps and blind spots I fell into, and move you toward a life directed with intentional joy.

Your life is not meant to be bland, boring, or depressing.
You were born for challenge, to find meaning, to experience bliss.
You are meant for more.

You exist because every ancestor before you survived long enough to pass the torch to *you*.

That makes you capable, creative, powerful—deeply human.

If that's not fun enough, then know this: you deserve a life
so extraordinary it needs made-up words to describe it—like
supercalifragilisticexpialidocious.

That's how I live.
And it's exactly what helped me turn my stories into digestible lessons for you.

And when I got scared by how ambitious this goal really was, I did what I'd conditioned myself to do:

I took action before I felt ready.

The result?

This book.
From me—to you.

THE PROMISE

This book breaks down the same 15-beat story structure Hollywood uses to create billion-dollar movies—and shows you how to use it to direct your life.

By the end of this book, you'll have the sequence and steps to create your own Director's Board—a physical board you can see, touch, and build scene by scene—giving you clarity, alignment tools, and the confidence to stop drifting and take the wheel.

You'll *know* what it takes to make your life better than any movie.

But this only works if you work it.
If you test the steps.
If you implement instead of just *knowing.*

And I get it. Right now, your life might feel rushed. Heavy. Predictable. Stressful. That's not failure, that's being human in the modern age.

So give yourself some grace and take it one step at a time. But with each step, I'm asking you to go all in and lean into the challenge ahead.

If you follow the map and complete the actions, you can upgrade your life and wake up most days with that "damn, it feels good to be a gangster" feeling.

Yeah, yeah, Tony. I've heard this before. The film metaphor is cute, but I'm an accountant, not a filmmaker. And my life still didn't improve!

That may be true—but if nothing changed, you weren't really committed.

You were dabbling.
Reading without implementing.
Wanting without deciding.
Hoping without building.

This book is different only if you are.

YOU HAVE THREE CHOICES

1. Stare at the blank page until someone drags you away to write on theirs.

2. Destroy every blank page you see.

3. Face the blank page every day—fearlessly, patiently, and with trust.

Write the story you've always wanted to live... *then live it.*

Most people don't face the blank page.
They avoid it.

They let someone else write their story.
They stay stuck in the same loops, the same excuses, the same distractions.

You're here because you're ready to take control of your life.

Some people have a problem with that word *control.*
So let's wipe the smudge off that lens.

When you try to control the external world—politics, other people's opinions, the outcomes you can't predict—you burn yourself out. You lose the energy and focus needed to move the needle where it actually matters.

When I talk about control, I mean mastering your inner world and the behaviors that flow from it.

Your impulses
Your judgment
Your comparisons

How you invest your time
How you show up for your family

What you consume and what you create
Your words

And that first moment in the morning—do you turn toward your phone or turn toward your partner?

No partner yet?

Then turn toward your day with purpose first.

That's the kind of control I'm talking about.
Not dominance—direction.

If you can focus on what you can control and accept what you cannot, then you're ready to learn what it really takes to become the Director of your life.

MY TRANSFORMATION

Today, I'm happy, *enthusiastic*, and fulfilled most of the time. I'm also a writer, film director, and keynote speaker—but that wasn't always my story.

My real job now is bringing my *best authentic self* to the occasion as often as possible… but in my late teens and early twenties, I was a petty thief, mumbling through life in self-pity and confusion. I was constantly seeking significance in all the wrong places.

I was too insecure to catch my dreams, so instead, I chased the fleeting high of feeling *important.* But it wasn't through growth or purpose. It was through stealing.

I wasn't numbing out the usual ways, but I was still addicted to self-loathing and the drama of my own mind. I was a nihilist caught in a cycle of temporary highs and spiraling lows.

Smash cut to now—my life looks completely different.

I actually like people, and *most* people like me (so I'm told). But I still come with a warning label.

I've guided countless creatives into their own spotlight, written seven feature film scripts, directed a plethora of projects, written this book, and spent about a year living throughout Southeast Asia.

That's where I found the love of my life—not a mermaid, legs and all—an island girl from the Philippines.

No one grabbed me and forced me to change. I wasn't rescued.

I stayed in the fight.

I kept searching, kept showing up—awkwardly, imperfectly—and over time, I evolved.

The same kid who once ran from conversations (*and girls)*, second-guessed himself constantly, over-analyzed everything, and hid a life he was ashamed of now speaks on stages with conviction, openly sharing the very story he once buried in silence.

WHY I BELIEVE IN YOU

I've watched people who once believed they were capped—emotionally, creatively, socially—step into entirely new versions of themselves.

Sometimes quietly.
Sometimes loudly.

Not overnight.
Not magically.

But through small *and* big, deliberate shifts in how they thought, acted, and chose.

Some were struggling, on the verge of burying themselves.
Some were doing "pretty good."
Some were alive, connected, chasing their dreams, and building flourishing relationships.

And every single one of them had another level available, whether they knew it or not.

That's what living your life better than any movie is really about.

Not fixing what's broken, but working with what you have and directing what's possible.

I'm not sharing what follows to boast.

I'm sharing it to show you what's possible when you commit to being the Director of your own life.

I've learned to:

- Experience joy every single day—even on the days I want to punch someone in the face.
- Express my love for the world, overcoming hesitation and inhibition—even on the days others want to punch *me* in the face.
- Live on my terms, free from the chains of past doubts and insecurities.
- Connect deeply with people who actually elevate me.
- Make time for what truly matters—one to three hours of laser focus on relationships and meaningful work most days.
- Transform life's random depressions into creative expressions.

Yeah, it's cliché, but it's true.

If I can go from a shy, self-deprecating, insecure thief to a confident, thriving creator, then I know you can break through your own barriers and embark on your own hero's journey too.

This is the elixir I'm offering you:
the mindset, the tools, and the system to direct your life.

You don't need unshakable self-belief to start this book.

You'll build it as we go.

But if you don't have any yet...

borrow mine for now.

All you have to do is commit.
Don't be interested. *Commit.*

YOUR TURN

What if you could live most days like a kid who can't hold a laugh in?
What if you were enthusiastic every day as if it were your first?

Imagine yourself in alignment with what truly matters to you—never holding back a smile, never dimming your light, living as a role model, fully connected to the universe.

When you live like this, people notice.
They'll say, *"What's wrong with this person? Why are they so energized and happy all the time? What are they up to?"*

Even when the storms hit.
Even when setbacks come.

This is how I aim to live.

I solve bigger puzzles with enthusiasm anyway.

Nearly every day, I give myself directives:

What could be exciting about today?
What can I make happen?
What's the one thing I must do?
How do I want to show up?

Life is a lot like directing a film—we make plans and set intentions, but we also need to stay open to what unfolds.

Sometimes we get what we call on set "happy accidents"—unplanned moments that make the final cut better than anything we scripted.

Every day, you can write scenes, cast characters, and choose where to focus the camera.

But people have a predicament—they let someone else call the shots. They zoom in on the negatives, let the wrong characters take center stage, and miss the beauty in their own story.

You're not here for that.

You're here because you're ready to create a life worth living—one filled with adventure, connection, growth, and meaning, damn it!

What's the thing that keeps people stuck in a below-average life they don't even enjoy?

They keep rewatching the same *bad film* over and over.
They forget that *they* choose the film, the genre, and how many times they watch it.

They don't commit to the work.
They don't follow through.

They don't read.
They don't give themselves grace.

Don't be like most people, or you'll get what most people have—an ordinary life as a background character directed by others.

YOUR NEW NARRATIVE

In filmmaking, we use beats to map out the story—moments that move the plot forward. Your life has beats too, and this book will guide you through yours.

What you're holding isn't theory.
It's a system forged from real stories, real struggle, and real transformation.

This is about cultivating the ultimate film called *Your Life.*
It can become the best you've ever experienced—or the worst.

Either way, you'll be replaying it until your last days.

So choose wisely.

You don't want to reach the end and whisper:
"Why did I make such a crappy film? What could I have become… if I had only made those edits?"

The best time to begin?
Yesterday.

The next best?
Today.
Right now.
Later means never.

It's time to commit.
It's time to write the story you want to live.
It's time to Direct Your Life.

YOUR PROLOGUE

The prologue of your life is never the whole story. It's the moment you discover your voice or realize you've been silenced. Either way, the next chapter is yours to write.

Your prologue isn't where you grew up. It isn't your past mistakes, your missed chances, or the dreams you put on hold. Your prologue is right now.

The moment you stop drifting, get present, and decide how the next chapter of your life will feel.

That choice begins the second you decide it does.

I remember the moment I learned this in real time.

Years ago, during a new era of my life, when I was trying to evolve but still tripping over old patterns, I was walking down the hallway of my tiny office, venting to a new friend. I don't even remember what I was complaining about. I just know I was frustrated and blurting out ridiculous obscenities.

He stood there listening.

Then he cut me off.

"Do you want to go out like this?"

"What?"

"If you died today, would you want to go out like this—complaining about stuff that doesn't matter?"

I stopped. Let out a long breath. Looked at him. Shook my head.

"That's sooooo good," I said, looking up as if the answer was on the ceiling.

That question became one of my go-to pattern interrupts.

It pulls me out of pointless venting.

Venting without a plan wastes time and drains the energy of everyone around you.

So the question is:

Do you want to go out like this?

Your prologue is the choice to stop drifting, get present, and allow the future to take shape.

HOW *YOU KNOW* YOU'RE NOT DIRECTING

Warning: Your ego is about to show itself. Suspend it.

- You wake up reacting instead of creating
- You let other people's plans fill your calendar
- You say "yes" out of fear instead of purpose
- You binge-watch lives instead of leading your own
- You talk about change more than you take action

These aren't flaws—they're signs you've forgotten you're the Director.
Let's fix that by getting you out of your head and into your body.

First, understand this:
If you're slouched, overly relaxed, or collapsed, you're in passive mode.
And passive mode doesn't create momentum.
You need to activate your nervous system into go mode.

Stand up.
If you can't stand, lift your chest.
Take a deep breath.
Move your body.
Shake out your hands.
Now add play.

Make a silly noise like a kid.
Say something out loud in a silly superhero voice:
"It's time to learn."

Let out a kiai like a martial artist before impact.
Clap your hands like an athlete about to enter the game.
Or, like we say on set before we roll camera:

"Here we go—pictures up!"

If this feels ridiculous, good.
That means you've been disconnected from playfulness for far too long.

These nervous-system triggers aren't gimmicks.
They shift you from reactive to proactive—from drifting to directing.

This is the charge you'll need from here on out. It's up to you to find your own power move so you can follow through with energy and delight.

Before every session, every chapter, every meaningful block of focus, reactivate. This is how you stay locked on the scenes that move your story forward, cut the negative dialogue from your script, and use your body the way a Director uses lighting to shape the mood of the entire set.

This isn't a read-for-pleasure book—*it's a direct-your-life script.*

You're not only the reader.
You're the Director.

Your new story begins now.

THE DIRECTOR'S BOARD

We're going analog.

You're going to build your *life-movie* beat by beat with real index cards—just like screenwriters do when mapping scenes that move a film forward.

It's old-school and it works.

What You Need:

Bulletin board · Index cards · Bold marker · Pen · Wall space

Your life is not a spreadsheet—*it's a story.*

As you plot what we call your *beats*, you'll start seeing your life with structure and clarity.

You'll know where you're headed and start living with cinematic momentum.

The moment you commit to this new role—Director of Your Life—your brain starts filtering for scenes, people, and opportunities that align.

This isn't metaphor.
There's science behind why this works.

Imagine you're a new filmmaker learning about dolly shots—when the camera glides in or out on a subject to intensify a moment. You think, *This is revolutionary. A game-changer.*

Then you rewatch films and start noticing it everywhere.
Movies. Television. Music videos. Commercials.

The technique was always there, but you didn't have the awareness to see it.

Once you learn it, you can't unsee it.

If you've read personal-development books before, you've probably heard of it—usually explained with some version of *"suddenly you see the red car everywhere."*

The same mechanism exists in your brain. It's called the Reticular Activating System (R.A.S.). It's the filter that determines what gets your attention and what gets ignored.

The moment you decide what you're aiming for—better health, deeper purpose, a creative project worth finishing—your brain starts tuning in to people, signals, and opportunities that support it. Most of them were already there. Now you notice them.

Focus on the wrong things, and your story feels scattered.
Focus *with intention*, and your story develops.

Whatever you consistently zoom in on becomes the film you're living inside.

Remember—*it's your R.A.S.*

YOUR FOUNDATION

This is where *thinking big picture* comes into play.

Before any great film gets made, the creator needs an overall sense of the story: its direction, its intention, its heartbeat.

Many master storytellers begin with two simple elements:

A compelling Title—one that whispers or screams the theme

A strong Logline—a one-sentence pitch that captures what the whole story is about

When you view your life through this lens, every choice becomes clearer.

YOUR TITLE

If your dream life were a movie, what would it be called?

Something that captures your journey, your essence, your fight.

Cinematic Examples:

My Past Does Not Equal My Future
For My Family
Breaking My Own Rules
From Shadows to Spotlight
No More Limiting BS

It can start as a working title and evolve as your story does.

YOUR LOGLINE

Think of it as your 30-second elevator pitch for your life—one or two sentences that sum up where you've been, what you've overcome, what you're about now, and where you want to go.

My Example:

Title: *Direct Your Life*

Logline: *A shy, dyslexic underdog battles fear, doubt, and self-sabotage until he rewrites his story, builds unshakable confidence, and steps into the spotlight—then guides others to do the same.*

Once you establish these, everything else—your goals, choices, and daily actions—starts aligning with the life-movie you're trying to make.

ACTION!

It's time to create your **Hero Card**—the anchor of your Director's Board.

This is the foundation. It captures who you are, what you're about, and the story you're committed to creating.

I know commitment isn't easy. When something matters, your ego, your doubts, and your old patterns all try to pull you back. I've started things I cared about, lost momentum, then "forgot about them," too.

That's exactly why these first steps are simple, doable, and momentum-building. Don't skip it.

It gets you warm.
It gets you moving.
It gets you directing.

Take out an index card, pen, and marker.

Here's the two-step sequence I want you to commit to right now:

1. **Create your Hero Card.**

   Write your Title and your Logline—your one-sentence life-movie description.

2. **Pin it on your Director's Board—front and center.**

   This is your first official take as the Director of your life.
   Start here, start now, and let this card set your story in motion.

This is the foundation for the 15 beats of your transformation we'll build together in this book.

Oh, and this should be fun.
Remember *fun*?

That thing you had as a kid before everything got too serious?

Well—this is it.

Fun. Creative. Playful. Meaningful.

Do it now.

BUILD YOUR DIRECTOR'S BOARD

COMPANION RESOURCES

To get the most out of this book, I've created powerful companion resources for you.

Readers who **pair this book with the audiobook and companion video training** often move faster and commit to following through on what matters most.

Access the full audiobook, companion video training, plus downloadable tools to help you apply what you learn immediately.

directyourlifebook.com/start

GET THE AUDIO BOOK FREE

Thank you for picking up this book. As a gift, I want to give you the full audiobook—**100% free**.

I narrated it myself so it feels like we're having a real conversation—Director to Director. (Well, I'll be doing all the talking… but you can pause me with one tap. If only real life worked that way.)

Listening while you drive, walk, or work out between reading chapters helps the ideas sink in and turns them into action.

It's not a droned-out audiobook. It's cinematic and built to reinforce what you're learning so you actually follow through.

GET THE COMPANION VIDEO TRAINING FREE

This short, 3-part video training gives you a *rolling start*—so when you open the book, you're already thinking like a Director.

This breaks down 3 key ideas:

Drifting VS Directing The mindset shift that changes everything	What a Director Board Is—how to set it up so you can design the life you want	How To Put It Into Action—applying the book for maximum impact

THE DiRECTOR'S ViEW

NON-NEGOTIABLES FOR A LIFE WORTH WATCHING

"Your philosophy creates your attitudes, your actions,
and your results. Those three things create your life."

—Jeff Olson, *The Slight Edge*

I've been fired from jobs more than once. Not because I lacked skill, but because I was ambitious in all the wrong ways.

I remember working as assistant for a production company when I made a rookie mistake. I was helping a big-time director they had brought in, and we were running casting sessions with actors. I operated the camera while the director worked with them. He was cool. We talked, and before he left he handed me his card.

A week later I emailed him about the upcoming shoot, thinking I had made a smart move.
I hadn't.

Word got back to the producers during a meeting.
Even though the director didn't mind the email, they were furious.

"I don't want some overly ambitious PA working with us. Blake, call him and let him go."

Blake, my thoughtful *brother-in-law*, was the one who got me the job. Now he had to be the one to fire me.

The call was embarrassing, but not devastating.
I didn't crumble, I took note.

I realized that ambition without strategy is chaos.
And chaos gets you fired.

Before you can direct your life, you need to understand the rules.
Most people think there are no rules—that's why they're losing.

You need to know the rules so you can deliberately break them.

I specialize in taking wild ideas and making them real—while building a life where fulfillment isn't delayed.

Decades of relentless trial and error gave me feedback, not theory.
Now I'm inviting you inside my head, not to admire it—to use it.

A Director's manual in hand.
In service of your creative life.

But don't start this journey unless you're ready to commit.

And you're ready when you step onto the film set of life—never before.

If you want to find meaning and bliss in your life, so it doesn't suck, you'll need to stop drifting and start directing.

That requires:

- Hyper-focus
- Doing hard things
- Finding joy in the process

Cut off all other options.

A single decision can change your day.
A deep commitment can change your life.

No dabblers allowed inside my mind.
Only Directors.

NON-NEGOTIABLE ONE

Focus On The Big Picture First

Directors don't just shoot scenes—they guide the entire story.

In life, that means living in alignment. Doing what matters. Making decisions that reflect who you truly are, and not what's easy in the moment.

Live with clarity. Lead with integrity. Remember: how you live one scene affects the next. And how you envision the next reflects the present one. Be intentional.

Continuously evolve.
Embrace challenges.
Learn from failure.

Commit to expanding your being—not because you need fixing, but because when you grow, you make progress. And when you make progress, you're happier!

Don't let your plot go stale.

Move Your Story Forward

When something unexpected happens on set, a great Director doesn't freeze—they adapt, pivot, and create something even better. Life is no different.

Don't wait for the perfect scene. Don't wish for a different script. Take what's in front of you and start making intentional edits.

Growth is the story. Whatever you focus on should move your story forward or develop your character—preferably both simultaneously.

Prepare thoroughly, stay adaptable, and be willing to take the leap. Nothing is set in stone until you say so. And even then.

Once you have the big picture and generate momentum, you must zoom in on what we call the dailies—your everyday scenes that shape your story.

The Director's Daily Practice:

- Build the habit of awareness via journaling
- Get wildly excited to meet new challenges
- Trade your expectations for appreciation
- Take bold, imperfect action
- Be radically open-minded and ready to learn
- Grow your confidence
- Admit when you're wrong, then correct it
- Lead with integrity
- Find humor in moments of frustration

That last one is a life saver. Think about a time you and someone else were sulking, glaring at each other, when suddenly your stomach growled like a cartoon bear. End of fight.

Once this mindset is in your bones, life gets better.

You won't just start things.
You'll finish them.
With clarity. With purpose.
With enthusiasm that no algorithm can touch.

NON-NEGOTIABLE TWO

Master Your Energy

None of these practices you'll be learning matters if you don't have the energy to execute.

You will never follow through on anything *long-term* unless your health is in check.

You can have the vision.
You can have the steps.
But without the energy, you will burn out.

This isn't about eating vegetables.
This is about real health.

Mind. Body. Spirit.
Lifelong mastery of energy, vitality, and mental strength.

I'm not going into a full health lesson here.
But I encourage you—make this the moment you get your health on track and turn it into a lifestyle.

My Health Journey—The Short Version

I was lucky. My father studied with Michio Kushi, a Japanese health expert, in the '70s and '80s. That passion trickled down early.

At twelve, while my friends poured sugary syrup onto pancakes, I added a few drops (I was the weird kid if you haven't already figured out). That same summer, I was doing a hundred push-ups a day, studying martial arts, and practicing splits between chairs like Jean-Claude Van Damme.

At sixteen, I read Fast Food Nation and declared war on processed junk—not to lose weight, but to feel like I could take on the world.

At twenty, I made a declaration: "I want to be able to perform handstands into my eighties."

Not for aesthetics. Okay, I'm human and I like to look good—but more importantly, I want the energy to explore, create, and evolve for as long as I'm alive.

Wait… how did I get into trouble in my teens and early twenties? This is some paradox tomfoolery, Tony. Health habits don't automatically equal emotional maturity.

Today, I'm grateful to feel more energetic and excited about life than ever. Not because I was perfect, but because I kept the slight edge.

Let food be the fuel to your clarity, focus, and stamina. What you eat is the energy you direct your life with. Put junk in, get junk scenes out.

I don't "cheat." I choose better fuel 85–90% of the time.

It's not about perfection or punishment.
It's about *consistency*.

And yes, I'll still grab pizza or dessert on those days, but I choose versions without refined sugar or endless additives as often as possible.

That mindset—fueling the work instead of soothing the moment—is what keeps the camera rolling.

When you get the call, do you have the energy to say yes?

Take a moment to assess how you feel right now.

Lively or lethargic?
Enthusiastic or exhausted?

Either one is an indication of how you've treated yourself over the last 72 hours—and the accumulation of the past few months.

That includes your mindset, exercise, diet, sleep, and relationships.

I believe everyone deserves—and is responsible—to live a full, spirited life to the best of their capabilities.

For yourself.
For your family.
For your work.
For your partner.
For your future.

Whether it's a walk, a conversation, a tough decision, or a new opportunity— life doesn't wait for perfect conditions.

It asks if you're ready.

The question isn't what you can do.
It's whether you're doing the best you can with what you have right now.

When the call comes, you don't need to be perfect.
But you do need to be able to step forward.

WHY IT MIGHT BE HARD TO FOLLOW THROUGH

If you're reading this and thinking,
"I know what to do… I just don't do it," or you've had to reread the last section because your focus keeps slipping,

I want you to hear this clearly:

It's not a willpower problem.
You are not lazy.
You are not broken.
It's not because "it runs in your family."

And you are definitely not a lost cause.

Sometimes what we label as a discipline problem is actually an energy problem.

Your ability to follow through, stay focused, feel motivated, or even feel excited about life is closely tied to how well your brain and body are producing and using key neurotransmitters and hormones.

So if you feel like lying on the couch watching reality TV, doom-scrolling on your phone, and hitting your bong between pizza bites instead of committing to your life's work, it's not a character flaw.

It's an energy issue.

When you identify what's off, you stop guessing. And when energy comes back online, momentum follows.

I don't want you reading this book thinking:

"I just can't focus."

"I'm not passionate about anything."

"Everyone else can do this except me."

If discipline keeps failing, don't quit on yourself.

Check your health before you wreck yourself.

Disclaimer: I'm not a medical professional, and nothing here is medical advice. This is for informational purposes only. Do your own research and consult a qualified professional when appropriate. Translation: Don't blindly follow anyone—especially me. Learn what works for you. Cut the rest.

NON-NEGOTIABLE THREE

Own Your Mindset

Here are the core philosophies that will keep you centered when the world tries to knock you out.

Memento Mori: Remember You Must Die

Remember, you must die.

Let that ring in your head—not to scare you, but to awaken you.
To shake you.
To remind you: LIVE NOW.

Yes, the inevitable can trigger doom and gloom thinking, but that mindset serves no one.

Focus on what makes you feel alive. Connected. Awake. This moment is a gift. Don't squander it on trivial time-wasters.

You will get sucked into others' agendas, emotions, and world distractions. We all do. But the more you train your awareness and commit to the Director's tools, the faster you'll pull yourself out.

Ever been in an argument where, halfway through, you forget what you're even arguing about? But pride keeps it going. The need to win, to be right. Time slips away. Emotions drain you. When it's over, you feel hollow.

You just lost time.
Time you will never get back.
And you let it happen.

That's when Memento Mori should be activated.

Pause, breathe, and ask: "Time is short. Life is precious. Are we going to waste it or live it?"

Recte Vivere: To Live Rightly

This concept is about living on your terms, in the right direction, with real happiness and strong relationships that last. It also means learning how to feel joy without needing proof from circumstances. Joy because you choose it, not because life handed you the perfect scene.

At twelve, on a flight with my amazing Aunt Terry—who surprised me with a trip to visit my cousins out of state—I sat next to a stranger shuffling cards.

As a shy kid, I observed everything. But as soon as I was amazed, my fear of conversation disappeared. I jumped in: "How did you do that?"

Most adults might think, "Here come the endless questions." But not this guy. He handed me the deck and taught me magic for the rest of the flight!

He saw a curious kid and thought, "Let's feed that flame." His name was David. He was living rightly. Not because anyone told him to, but because he chose to give.

That moment changed the trajectory of my life. Magic eventually led me to advance my social skills and break past my self-limitations. It also helped me retain my kid-like qualities and probably kept me from getting completely sucked into the dark side.

David taught me that living rightly isn't complicated—it's noticing the moment you could hold back, and choosing instead to give your presence.

Amor Fati: Love Your Fate

When living rightly collides with fate, that's when the hardest principle comes into play...

"Not to merely accept your fate, but to love it."

Not tolerating. Not surviving. Loving.

Years ago, I took on a filmmaking project for one of the largest companies in Japan. We had a contract, vision, and a big budget. I poured months into crafting something cinematic and meaningful.

Near final delivery, they loved everything except the animation. Instead of allowing revisions, they shut the door. "We're moving on." No explanation. No remaining balance.

I offered to rework the edit. Asked what wasn't working. Instead of feedback, I got excuses, then silence.

I had to accept the fate. I sued. I hated the idea of months in downtown LA courtrooms, but I wasn't standing up for myself—I was standing up for every creative who's been disrespected or dismissed.

With Amor Fati in mind, I did my best to enjoy the process. I even brought my wife on filing days, turning chaos into downtown dates.

I won the case and walked away with clarity and the funds they owed—not bitterness. I didn't smear them online or let it poison my art. I used it as fuel.

That legal mess taught me how to protect my value, communicate boundaries, and lead my business professionally—not desperately.

Amor Fati isn't about pretending to like pain. It's about staying creative through it, reframing every hit as growth, every detour as discovery, and every fear as a cue for action.

Life will always have ups and downs. When you embrace Amor Fati, you learn to love the journey—all of it. You find wisdom in struggle, creativity in chaos, competence in challenges.

You embrace the suck.

The key isn't to pretend hardships don't affect you. It's to meet them head-on, and then make the best of what's in your hands. Love the cards you've been dealt, and play them with everything you've got.

Life will never hand you the perfect scene, but the greats don't wait for it. They shoot anyway.

These principles take repetition, commitment, and willingness to adjust when life yells "Cut!"

But they're worth it. If you lean in, experiment, and condition them, you'll begin moving through life differently—less reactive, more deliberate. Less bitter, more creative.

You can't control fate, but you can control your response to it.

And that is enough.

ACT I
WRITE YOUR STORY

> "The only thing keeping you from what you want
> is your story about why you can't have it."
>
> —Tony Robbins

BEAT 1

YOUR REALiTY

"Your worst sin is that you betrayed and
destroyed yourself for nothing."

—Fyodor Dostoevsky

My life was a tightrope walk—literally.

Los Angeles. Night. 2007. I parked my car in the shadows between two apartment buildings and the Freeway. Then I climbed a thirteen-foot wall and balanced on a six-inch ledge, prowling low like a cat obsessed with its prey—the next piece of property I could steal.

I thought the world didn't understand me. I was angry, lonely, lost, and broke. On top of that, I was a hopeless romantic who didn't party or really socialize. My vice was sneaking around and testing what I could get away with. It gave me a false sense of significance.

Out of the corner of my eye, I caught a flicker of light. A family was having dinner on the second floor of an apartment across the way. A simple, peaceful scene. But it hit me hard.

I'm alone. On a freeway wall. At night. Stealing.

Not to feed a family, but out of resentment, spite, and lack. A silent tantrum born of emotional immaturity—unprocessed and unaware.

I didn't know self-love yet. I didn't know that my weirdness was a superpower. I only knew I was different, and I leaned too far into that difference.

Self-inflicted exile.
I was letting bitterness direct my life.

I flashed back to fifth grade.

My teacher scorned me for acting out.
She hovered over me in front of the class, face blank with no remorse, and mocked:

"You're a troublemaker. Watch out. One day you'll grow up with problems and say, 'darn, back on the streets again.'"

Balancing my life on that freeway wall, staring at that family through their window, I had an epiphany.

I'm digging an early grave, betraying myself for nothing. Destroying my future in the present.

What I really wanted was connection.

And to become a man of integrity—someone who only took what he earned. Nothing more, nothing less.

I climbed back down. As the light hit my face, something inside me shifted. I wasn't numb anymore. I was aware. Awake for the first time.

That night set me on a new path: personal growth, creativity, and transformation.

I went back home to my garage. If you peeked in, you'd see me scribbling under the faint glow of an overhead light—stacks of journals and crumpled pages surrounding me. Lyrics, film ideas, existential questions, monologues. It was messy, raw, and imperfect, but it saved me.

I started chipping away at the hardened marble that had formed around my true self. I found mentors. I made new friends. I got clarity. And most importantly, I found direction.

That moment on the wall—cold, isolated, and desperate—was my *Opening Image.*

It was the first time I officially and *consciously* stepped into the role of Director.

THE OPENING IMAGE

That night taught me something crucial about human nature. We all want the same things: connection, love, purpose, and growth. But when we feel unworthy, we act out in our own negative ways to seek significance.

My "freeway wall" was literal theft. Yours is probably different. Maybe you seek significance through perfectionism, people-pleasing, workaholism, or staying invisible. But we all have our version of prowling on a ledge in the dark.

What's your freeway wall? What's your family-in-the-window moment, the role model in the distance showing you what connection actually looks like?

You might be living on autopilot and entertaining bad behavior because you don't know your purpose yet—or you've lost track of it—or maybe even forgotten what your passions are. Most people go through the motions.

That's not living.

Why?

Fear.

You already know this.

Deep down, you're afraid you're not enough. You're afraid of looking foolish. You're afraid that you won't be liked or loved. You fear judgment and comparison. Yet, you subject yourself to it for hours every day on social media.

It's deeply ingrained in our biology and subconscious. Evolution wired us that way to avoid danger.

But the problem is that these modern fears are not life-threatening dangers.

We've been tricked.

Most of those fears are false takes. In filmmaking, a false take is when we mess up before the camera even rolls and we have to reset. That's what limiting beliefs are: never-ending false takes that never become real scenes.

And those false takes drain your life force.

Some researchers argue we're born with only two primal fears:

Fear of falling
Fear of loud noises

Everything else was learned or burned into us by our environment, parents, peers, the government, and the media.

When you're afraid, the secret is to do it anyway.

You might know this. But again, knowing isn't enough. This has to live in your body and in your soul.

Remember, it's all right to feel embarrassed—I recommend it. That discomfort? That's growth. I've been embarrassed so many times it feels like a second home. It always moved me forward.

When you embrace vulnerability, you'll start choosing it. Why? Because it's the key to expanding your being.

Everything you've reflected on—your fears, your freeway wall, your patterns—is part of your Opening Image. Great films start with an Opening Image, the first snapshot of who a character is before their transformation begins.

What's your Opening Image?

Don't try to look perfect. Get real. That's your power.

You don't have to hit rock bottom to begin. You can decide that now is your starting point.

DIRECTOR'S COMMENTARY

Take a look in the mirror. What's your reality?

Health, career, relationships, passion—it's all part of your story.

Stop living on autopilot.
Hit pause.
Reset.

Decide what story you actually want to tell next.

Make health your foundation. Your health isn't just fuel—it's the camera battery for your life's big shoot. Without it, you can't power through to the next scene.

Remember: don't judge yourself. Observe the facts. Then start.

KEY TAKEAWAYS

- Self-awareness is your first scene.
- Vulnerability creates clarity.
- Don't get stuck in false takes—they keep you from the real scene.
- Your health and honesty are your lenses—keep them clean.

ACTION!

I know you have a life. I know there are only twenty-four hours in a day. But if you take fifteen minutes right now to complete the action step below, you'll trigger a genuine time reset.

You'll realign, re-center, and reclaim where your energy goes—because everyone has fifteen minutes for the life they actually want.

Commit to completing this beat, and you'll create momentum that carries you through the week.

Grab a blank index card and set it up like.
Complete it, and then pin it underneath your Hero Card.

If you don't have your Hero Card yet—STOP. Go back to the Prologue and create it now. This system doesn't work without it.

Once you've set your Opening Image, we cut to the next scene—the central question your life is built to answer.

You are the writer and the Director.
Get to it.

BEAT 1—MY REALITY

Opening Image
My current reality:

____

____

Metaphor
The story I'm telling myself about life right now is:
Example: "Life is hell" / "Life is a puzzle"

____

____

Health Check
Right now, I'm:
☐ Thriving ☐ Surviving

Honesty Scale
On a scale of 1–10, how honest was I just now?
__ / 10

BEAT 2

THE HEART OF YOUR STORY

"Come on, Suriano! Head up! This is when
your training begins—when you want to give up!"

—Mr. Goodwin, Kyo Sa Nim (교사님)

I was on the red and blue training mat,
exhausted, barely able to stand.

"Front kick, double punch!"
"Front kick, double punch!"
"Other side!"

Sweat stung my eyes, running down like a faucet on top of my head. It took every ounce I had to complete the moves.

I finally finished the grueling set of drills and staggered back to my starting point. Class was about to end.

"Final drill. Frog leaps forward! Bear crawl backward. Twenty reps. Begin!"

I couldn't believe it. More? There were only two minutes left in class.

I leaned on my knees, head down.
I wanted to quit.

I wanted to grab some water, but there was a strict no-water rule to build stamina. We drank before and after—never during.

"Head up, Suriano!"

I lifted my head slowly.

"I thought we were done," I said, out of breath.

"This is where your training begins!"

I wanted to be the best I could, for myself, sure, but even more for my Kyo Sa Nim. I've always respected martial arts and trained throughout most of my life. If he believed I had more left in me, then I must have it *somewhere*.

"Come on, Suriano!"

I pushed. Hard. I finished his training. I probably looked like I took an elephant tranquilizer and was learning to play hopscotch, but I finished.

My lungs burned. My body ached. I wanted water, but more than that, I wanted growth.

I caught something powerful during that training:

- Others can believe in you more than you believe in yourself—and their conviction becomes fuel.
- When you think you can't go any further, you can.
- Breaking through is painful, but worth it.

That was the day I discovered one of my core themes:

My limits are my lies.

I've carried that theme with me ever since. It has helped me push through moments in life where fear, doubt, or the easy way out tried to hold me back.

My Kyo Sa Nim's external belief became my internal operating system. That's how powerful a clear theme can be.

Modern psychology backs up what my instructor taught me on that mat: belief—whether it comes from others or from a theme you choose—rewires how you act under pressure and over time.

Your theme becomes your fuel because identity isn't fixed; it's built through repetition, reflection, and reinforcement.

Research inspired by psychologist Carol Dweck, PhD, and her book *Mindset: The New Psychology of Success* shows this at a neurological level. Participants who believed they could grow showed stronger brain engagement after mistakes—their minds stayed online, curious, adaptive, ready to learn. Those with a fixed mindset mentally checked out the moment they slipped.

Across long-term studies, adults who hold growth-based beliefs continue to strengthen skills, adapt faster, and reinvent themselves.

I loved her book.

There are many moments worth underlining, but one section struck a deep chord for me:

Mindsets are just beliefs. They're powerful beliefs—but they're just something in your mind, and you can change your mind. The view you adopt for yourself profoundly affects the way you lead your life. It can determine whether you become the person you want to be and whether you accomplish the things you value.

Your brain is not done.
Your identity is not fixed.
Belief isn't motivational. It's the operating system shaping your future.

THE HARSH QUESTIONS

When was the last time you gave up too soon and took the easy way out?

When did you let someone's careless remark hijack your whole day?

When did you scroll for hours on social media, comparing butts and Ferraris instead of creating?

When did you waste hours watching negative news that left you emptier than a popcorn bucket after a movie marathon on your cheat day?

Every time you do, you hand over your power. You trade gold for pennies. You bleed energy into trivialities instead of choosing a theme that could have shaped you.

If that makes you feel uncomfortable, good. I'm okay with inducing an uncomfortable feeling in this moment to lead you into better ones in the future.

Here's the biggest distraction of all: wearing someone else's name on your back, cheering for a team you'll never play for—that's not fulfillment, that's spectating. Fulfillment comes when you stop watching and start playing your own game.

And if you're wondering whether that was a metaphor or if I'm talking about watching sports. I'm talking about both.

I respect extraordinary people, and I enjoy witnessing mastery.
But I don't let cheap doses of "secondhand dopamine" replace the work required to earn my own fulfillment.

Your greatest victory will never come from the sidelines. It will come from directing your own story.

The harsh questions sting and that's the point.
Because the toughest opponent you'll ever battle wears your face, speaks in your voice, and knows every weakness you have.
Beat that enemy, and every other battle becomes easier.

When the inner critic tells you to give in, keep your head up.
Stop spectating and start directing.

This is when your training begins.

FRAME YOURSELF AS THE HERO

In martial arts, animal forms are studied for a reason. Each has its strength. The crane teaches balance, the tiger embodies power, the snake flows with adaptability. A tiger doesn't envy a crane's wings, and a crane doesn't try to strike like a tiger. Each rules its own domain, and so should you.

Comparison only blinds you to your natural power.
Then you lose your target, your speed, and your progress.

"If you put limits on what you do,
it spreads into your work and into your
life. There are no limits—only plateaus.
And you must not stay there."

—Bruce Lee

Your future isn't written by your conditions, it's directed by your decisions.
And strong decisions are made when you're feeling strong.

Frame yourself as the human being you are—the hero of your story.

Stand tall.
Put your hands on your hips and breathe like a superhero.
Do this for two minutes.

Your brain reads the posture as power, ready for what's next.

Research shows this posture increases your likelihood of taking action and reduces stress.

Look at the flip side: if you're slouched on the couch, eating ultra-processed food with a blank stare while watching reality-TV nothingness, do you feel like training for a marathon?

Your physiology communicates readiness to your brain.
Change your posture, change your possibilities.

You can't create an outstanding life from a low-energy state. You can be a Ferrari, but without fuel, you're not going anywhere—you're stuck.

FIND YOUR THEME

In film scripts, soon after the Opening Image comes the Theme, the part of the story that lays the groundwork for everything ahead.

Remember from Beat 1 when I was that self-loathing nihilist on the freeway wall? That was me stuck in the wrong genre. Living in drama and horror.

The moment I chose comedy and adventure as my genres?
Everything shifted.

Now it's time to map out the scenes of your life, define your genre, and start shaping your story.

Choose Your Genre

A great film usually sticks to one genre. Life's different. We cycle through multiple, sometimes in a single day. But if you position yourself and focus on your main one, when the harder genres sneak in (and they will), you'll be ready.

Don't choose drama, horror, war, or film noir. They'll find you anyway.

Instead, pick a genre that excites you to live in it:

Comedy—finding humor and lightness in daily experiences

Romance—focusing on connection and relationships

Mystery—approaching life with curiosity and discovery

Fantasy—embracing imagination and possibility

Musical—living with rhythm, creativity, and expression

Experimental—constantly trying new approaches and perspectives

These set you up for energy, happiness, growth, and fulfillment.

Choose Your Role

As a Director, you get to choose who plays which role in your film. And as the actor, you bring that role to life. The moment you claim both seats— Director and Performer—you stop waiting and start creating your destiny.

Throughout life, you shift roles, but the moment you decide you're the main character and *not a background actor*, everything changes.

There's a song I love by '80s band Oingo Boingo that asks something powerful: "Who do you want to be today?"

That question is necessary to ask daily if you want to lead a life worth living. It's a reminder that you always have a choice. Every single day, you get to decide who you're becoming.

DIRECTOR'S COMMENTARY

If you don't have a theme for your life, you're not directing—you're drifting.

When that happens, your mood dictates your actions and distractions devour your time.

You need a well-thought-out life philosophy that acts as your compass. Without it, you don't just wander the forest; you walk in circles, get exhausted, and eventually become food for a man-eating Kodiak bear.

Dark but true.

That's why every great film has a central theme—the big idea that drives the story. It's what the audience walks away with, the message underneath all the action.

Movie Examples:

The Matrix—"Free your mind."

Dead Poets Society—"Carpe diem. Seize the day."

Finding Nemo—"Just keep swimming."

It's okay if you never set a theme for your life.
Schools don't teach this stuff.
But today is the day you start.

KEY TAKEAWAYS

- Your theme becomes your operating system when decisions get hard.
- It doesn't have to be original, it has to be yours.
- Test it: does saying it out loud make you stand taller?

ACTION!

This should only take you five minutes. You've already lived through a lot. Now you're pulling the meaning out of it. Grab a blank index card and get to work.

When you finish, pin it under Your Reality Card from Beat 1. From this point on, every decision is filtered through this lens. Your life-movie has its heart. The story is officially in motion.

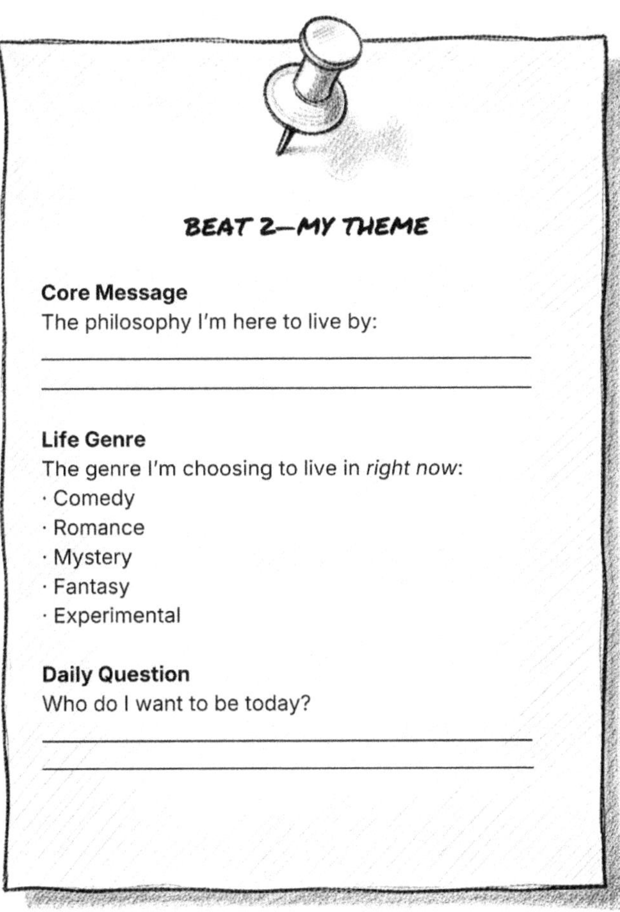

BEAT 3

UNDERSTAND YOUR WORLD

"The unexamined life is not worth living."

—Socrates

Comfort is dangerous. Complacency is lethal.

Benny Bing was a good guy once. Small-time wise guy, sure—but loyal, sharp, and hungry. He'd worked his way up from running numbers to managing a piece of the action at Dino's Bar & Grill. Nice steady income, respect from the neighborhood, and a comfortable routine that felt like paradise.

"This is the life," Benny would say, lighting his morning cigar behind the bar. No boss breathing down his neck. No real pressure. Just collect the weekly take, keep the peace, and enjoy the good life.

But little by little, the heat started to rise.

He stopped showing up early.
Started cutting corners.
Talking down to people he once called friends.
A free drink here, a little skim there.
He told himself it was nothing. Just perks of seniority.

Then the new crew moved in from the east side.
His regulars got jumpy.
The money dipped, barely noticeable at first.
But Benny had already lost his edge.

Benny was like a frog slowly being boiled.

By the time the water was hot enough to burn, he couldn't climb out.

One morning, they found him floating in the harbor—another man cooked by comfort, undone by his own slow decline.

Don't be Benny Bing.

That's the ordinary world in action—mafia-style: we get comfortable in environments that slowly kill our potential. We don't even notice the danger because it creeps in degree by degree.

Most people are living like Benny. They think they're in control, but really they're simmering in the slow boil of mediocrity until it kills them. Silently quitting.

PREVIOUSLY ON YOUR TRANSFORMATION…

You've discovered your Opening Image, the honest snapshot of where you are right now. You've identified your Theme, the core message driving your story forward. You've chosen your genre and started asking yourself daily, "Who do you want to be today?"

Now comes the crucial next step: understanding the world you're operating in.

You can have a powerful theme, but if you're not aware of your current environment, you'll end up like Benny Bing—comfortable and declining until you're dead.

That's what happens when you stay on autopilot too long and slip into a role that keeps you stuck. It happens to everyone. Periodically, you must check your character arc and decide if it still serves the story.

What role are you playing?

KNOW YOUR ROLE

On a film set, there are a handful of easy-to-spot roles. Some are background noise, some are supporting players, some execute brilliantly, and some take the lead.

In your life story, you're already playing one of these roles—whether you realize it or not. The question is: are you satisfied with your current role, or is it time to step into a bigger one?

THE EXTRA

Another background character in their own life. No lines. No impact. Going through the motions on autopilot.

Their Story:

- Hit 18, got an entry-level job, never looked for another
- Accidentally had kids—or didn't—and still stuck in the same routine
- Gets intoxicated on weekends, hates Mondays
- Thinks high school was the glory days

Theme: Drifting without direction, excitement, or ambition

THE STAND-IN

Fills different roles, experiments, but never fully steps into the spotlight.

Their Story:

- Explored jobs after 18, but still feels stuck in the same routine

- Responsible, raising a happy family—or still figuring out balance
- Flexible job with decent pay
- Loves dreaming and researching, but rarely takes action
- Wants more but lacks the confidence to go for it
- Mentally drained from menial, momentum-killing tasks

Theme: Wants more but is stuck in "someday" mode

THE ACTOR

A skilled performer who's earned their place but still reading from someone else's script.

Their Story:

- Followed the script after 18 with purpose
- Took direction well, earned accomplishments
- Applause for their work, but big dreams kept quiet
- Balances career and personal life
- Secretly waits for "discovery" instead of taking ownership
- Executes brilliantly but hesitates to lead their own vision

Theme: Excellence without ownership leads to a plateau

THE DIRECTOR

Who You Deserve to Be

The visionary who leads with purpose and never waits for permission.

Their Story:

- Followed passions, pursued goals with relentless focus
- Completed dozens of significant projects—always aiming for the moon
- Committed to continuous growth and learning
- Balances career and relationships without losing sight of priorities
- Confident, resourceful, and willing to ask for help
- Shapes the world to match their vision instead of waiting around
- Creates action that inspires
- Owns mistakes and course-corrects with humility

Theme: Life is a living, breathing film—sometimes comedy, sometimes drama—and you're either in the audience or directing the scene

These roles are indicators of how you've been playing your life so far. Call it what it is—without judgment, but with awareness.

I've personally played every one of them. That's why I have daily practices to keep myself directing. Left unchecked, we drift back into the less thrilling roles. Autopilot. Sleepwalking through scenes we never consciously chose.

Here's a framework designed to jolt you awake so you don't end up like Benny Bing, burning up in the wrong genre.

O.R.D.I.N.A.R.Y.

Most acronyms are designed to help you remember what to pursue. This one is the opposite. It represents everything you should *avoid* so you don't end up stuck in the ordinary world.

Picture the movie nobody wants to watch:

O—Ordinary

No defining characteristics. No passion. Just blending in.

R—Redundant

The same scenes repeat. No growth. No evolution.

D—Dreadful

Even you check out of your own life. The energy is flat.

I—Irrelevant

The story doesn't matter—least of all to you.

N—Numb

No emotional stakes. No urgency. Just autopilot.

A—Artificial

Everything feels staged. Forced. Like bad acting.

R—Reluctant

Every call to adventure is postponed. "Someday" becomes never.

Y—Yawn-Inducing

Even the soundtrack falls asleep.

This is the movie most people accidentally star in. Don't let it be yours.

AUDIT YOUR LIFE

A Director is responsible for everything that shows up on set and what makes it into the frame.

Many people—even the ones who look like they have it together—let life just happen to them. Days blur into years, and suddenly they're asking: "What even happened this last decade?"

Tony Robbins, world-renowned results coach, says: "Success in life is 80% psychology and 20% skill." I've trained with Tony twice at his Unleash the

Power Within events, and his psychology-first approach transformed how I see personal growth.

That means in order to change your life into the Academy Award-winning film you envision, you need to examine your mindset.

Check Your BS (Belief System)

- A belief is something you repeat until it becomes conviction
- Transformation begins when your actions align with the person you're evolving into
- When that alignment clicks, it seeps all the way into your biochemistry
- The big picture is ongoing mastery

This isn't just about setting goals, it's about rewiring your very essence. And once you do that, everything else falls into place.

"One of the great things about being a director as a life choice is that it can never be mastered. Every story is its own kind of expedition, with its own set of challenges."

—Ron Howard, Film Director

THE FOUR WORLDS

HEALTH

If you're going to take control of your life, you must first take control of your health.

Are you thriving with energy like a lion—king of your own jungle—or sluggishly waddling through life like a tired, overfed penguin who forgot how to swim?

When you eat poorly, you feel poorly.

And when your energy is low, do you really feel like taking the hard, rewarding actions necessary to create the life you want? Of course not.

Get your health in check or it's checkmate for your life ambitions.

PEOPLE

If you surround yourself with people who gossip, eat poorly, and lack ambition, you'll end up doing the same.

Have you heard the crab analogy?

When one crab tries to climb out of the bucket, the others pull it back down.

Same with people.

Fear and insecurity can make them afraid they'll lose you if you succeed—or worse, your courage reminds them they don't have any.

If you don't go after your dreams, it quietly reassures them that they don't have to go after theirs either.

But there's another kind of resistance that looks different.

Some people aren't trying to hold you back, they're trying to protect you. They worry about rent, stability, and whether you'll be okay if things don't work out. That concern often comes from love, not limitation.

The difference matters.

Fear-driven control still limits your growth even when it's well-intended.

Keep the empowering people close.

Listen respectfully to concern but don't let it override your calling.

And keep true energy vampires at a distance.

MENTAL

Your mindset drives the majority of your results.

When your thoughts, beliefs, and internal dialogue are aligned, you think clearly and feel connected to something bigger than momentary emotion.

That sense of clarity, meaning, and inner steadiness is what people often call *spiritual*.

I call it being connected.

When your health and relationships are strong, your mental state clicks into alignment.

If one is out of balance, it's like trying to shoot a film with a cracked lens. You might capture something, but it's going to be distorted and look like crap.

ENVIRONMENT

As peak performance expert Ed Mylett says, it's not just about the mental—it's about the environMENTAL.

He's right. Your environment either inspires you or conspires against you, and it all starts at home.

When I was a kid, my room was controlled chaos—alien posters, skateboard memorabilia, *The Simpsons* bedspread. I even had a "memento mori" section: a closet I painted black, filled with skeletal art, a possum hand bone, a metal skull, and my knives. Call me weird, but I thought it was the coolest.

My mom gave me space to explore, express, and be unapologetically myself. Her openness made room for my curiosity.

If you grew up with parents who were strict or closed off, I'm truly sorry. But you're an adult now and you get to choose what kind of environment you live in going forward.

My environment was fun, but it was random chaos.
I carried that scattered energy into my early twenties.

Now? My bedroom is intentionally minimal with white walls for pure rest. No, I don't sleep in a mental ward. I sleep in peace.

But my office is my creative playground. My walls carry the words I live by: "Everything you want is on the other side of uncomfortable action" and "The quality of your confidence is the quality of your life."

My favorite corner—my magician zone—is stacked with my beloved cards and coins where I make things disappear... like my free time.

But it also buys me curiosity and awareness.

Closing Shot

Before we wrap this scene, here's something that should land like a punch in the gut.

Palliative caregiver Bronnie Ware spent years documenting the top regrets of the dying. The same five surfaced again and again:

"I wish I'd had the courage to live a life true to myself, not the life others expected of me."

"I wish I hadn't worked so hard."

"I wish I had the courage to express my feelings."

"I wish I had stayed in touch with my friends."

"I wish I had let myself be happier."

Those aren't random regrets. They're warnings.

Every unchecked area you audited—health, people, mental state, environment—can quietly lead you straight to regret if you don't course-correct now.

Don't get to the final scene in your life and wish you prioritized what matters.

Now here's the challenge.

I almost left this next part out of the book.
But the power of crusade compels me.

Simple.
Difficult.
Eye-opening.

For the next 7 days, go on a no-news diet.

Wait, what?
This will help you prioritize the four worlds we discussed.

If that feels extreme, ask yourself this:

When was the last time you watched the news and felt refreshed, hopeful, and ready to live a meaningful life?

Exactly.

The news isn't designed to inform you—it's designed to hook you *then shock you*. There's a saying in the industry: *if it bleeds, it leads.* Fear keeps attention. Attention sells ads.

And the cost?
Your peace. Your focus. Your energy.

For seven days:

- Delete news apps or set them to local emergency alerts only
- Don't watch it at home, the gym, or restaurants
- If something truly important happens, you'll hear about it through people, not panic

You won't miss anything that actually serves your life.
But you *will* get time, clarity, and emotional bandwidth back.

If you want to go one step further, notice what else drains you:

Violent content. Doom-scrolling. Self-degrading entertainment. Anything that leaves you heavier than when you started.

Cut it for a week as a reset.

I haven't watched the news in over 22 years. My life didn't shrink—it expanded. I didn't miss out on meaning. I found more of it.

Okay fine. I lied a little.

I technically get *some* "news" through *South Park*, the animated satirical show.

Why? Because it processes what's happening in the world through humor, absurdity, and perspective. I end up laughing instead of spiraling. Laughter releases endorphins, reduces stress, and restores clarity. That matters.

If you're someone who watches the news daily and you take this challenge, you'll notice something fast:

The news behaves like a drama drug—you'll be itching for a fix.

That's not weakness—it's biology. Your brain prioritizes negativity because it interprets it as potential threat. It thinks paying attention keeps you safe. But not everything that's loud, urgent, or frightening deserves your focus.

Just because something *grabs* your attention doesn't mean it *earns* it.

For seven days, notice what happens when you stop feeding that loop. Notice how your energy shifts. Notice what you suddenly have the bandwidth to care about again.

If someone tries to pull you into news chatter, borrow my line:

"I know you're passionate about this, but can we talk about something more uplifting?"

Protect your peace and guard your energy.

You're directing a life here—*your life.*

Don't wait until your final scene to wish you'd changed the script.
Don't become that regret statistic.

And whatever you do, don't be Benny Bing.

DIRECTOR'S COMMENTARY

Your setup should be fun, because if it's boring, your life will be too. You've heard of the Sunday Scaries—that cute phrase people use when they really mean they hate Monday. But that pit-in-your-stomach dread isn't cute at all. It's a symptom of misalignment.

Obliterate the Sunday Scaries. Build a world you're excited to wake up to, whether the day ahead is hard, easy, or messy. Remember: your space should make you feel like you're already on set for the life-movie you're creating.

KEY TAKEAWAYS

- You're already playing a role (Extra, Stand-In, Actor, or Director) so you'd better know which one you are.
- Your Four Worlds (Health, People, Mental, Environment) either support or sabotage your story.
- Environment isn't decoration—it either inspires you or conspires against you.

ACTION!

Time to audit your life.

Grab a blank index card and describe your current world—the good, the bad, and the uncomfortable. Imagine the camera panning across your life right now. Are you fueling the life you want—or surviving on convenience and processed junk? Are the people closest to you lifting you—or dragging you into a bucket of crusty crabs? Is your mindset aligned with growth—or drifting in O.R.D.I.N.A.R.Y. thinking? Does your space inspire creativity—or conspire against your dreams?

If you're thinking, "Tony, I have money stress," I've been there. But money pressure is usually a symptom, not the root.

Declare this the moment you improve your world. Awareness without action is just expensive therapy.

Finish your card. Pin it on your Director's Board.

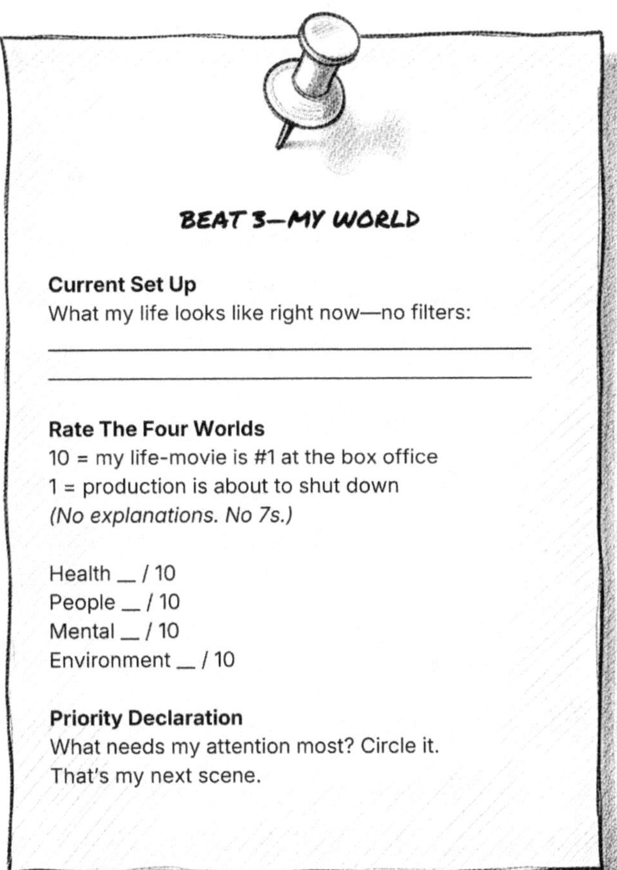

BEAT 4
YOUR WAKE-UP CALL

"This is the only moment you have.
This is your moment. Don't waste it."

—Personal Incantation

Most people don't miss their wake-up call.
They just don't recognize it because they
never decided who they're becoming.

You've already checked your reality, chosen a theme, and examined your world. So when the fork in the road appears, you won't ask which way to go.

You'll know.

THE CALL

In film, the call is referred to as the inciting incident—the moment that sets everything in motion.

It might arrive as new love, a brutal breakup, or that soul-crushing phone call. Maybe someone close passes away. Maybe your unhealthy lifestyle finally catches up. Perhaps someone needs your help and you're compelled to drop everything. Or maybe you realize you can't stay in the cutthroat Los Angeles another second and you move to the Philippines.

Whatever form it takes, the call should scare the hell out of you.

At first, most heroes refuse the call. That's the old brain in survival mode, avoiding discomfort at all costs.

This is it. You are the hero of your own film. Sometimes you choose to accept the call. Sometimes it's a shove—a crisis that leaves you no choice.

Either way, that's the threshold—the moment you step into the New World.

Congratulations: Most Never Get This Far

I'm pausing to give you recognition: you're still here. You've read, reflected, written on cards, maybe even hung up a dedicated Director's Board on your wall.

You're proving you're not "most people." You're answering the call.

If you were in person with me, I would knight you with an official Director's hat right now.

Now would be a great time to do a 1–2 minute stretch, grab some water, and get ready because the call is serious business.

It's nearly killed me several times.

But it's worth it every time.

Magic was calling my name.

But it came in a text from a new friend: "Hey man, this big company is looking for a stage magician. Should I let them know about you?"

Though I had been performing walk-around magic professionally, I had never done a stage show. Doubt kicked me in the head:

What if I can't create a show long enough? What if they find out I've never done a stage show? What if I say no and miss my moment?

Luckily, my conditioning to say yes to scary things showed up. Three shows a day, four days in a row. A real stage. A large audience.

I said yes!

I prepped, auditioned, and booked the gig.

Then I got sick. Not just sick—my body was wrecked and I was in major pain. Looking back, I realize it wasn't illness. It was the stress of wanting so badly to succeed, and the enormity of the event itself.

There's a verse that says, "Where there is no vision, the people perish." I had vision—maybe too much of it. The problem? I'd attached myself to the outcome instead of being present in the moment. That attachment nearly broke my spirit.

But mid-performance, I caught myself in the act. I snapped into being there for the audience. As the saying goes, *the show must go on.*

I pushed through all twelve shows, improvising a finale where snow fell as a magical flourish. The audience loved it. I was drained, but I finished strong. And no one knew I was sick.

Now I see it for what it was: a test. And I over-performed. Everything since has felt easier by comparison.

This was pressure. The kind we'll really explore in Beat 10. But for now, just know: when you answer the call, life tests whether you mean it.

Psychologists call this "stress inoculation"—facing controlled challenges builds resilience for future obstacles.

And there will always be future obstacles.

This is why we embrace the call: every challenge brings us wisdom that ripples out to those around us.

THE CATALYST COMPASS

The Catalyst Compass is the pull toward what's truly calling you, not the noise trying to distract you.

It's your True North—the path that's both exciting *and* a little scary, because it stretches you.

If you took the seven-day no-news challenge back in Beat 3, you've already felt what emerges when the noise drops away. Now let's sharpen that focus.

Here's how to recognize when something is truly calling you versus just noise:

True North

Exciting + Scary

Adventure.

Love.

Creative risk.

Contribution.

Truth-telling.

Growth.

A dream that won't leave you alone.

These are the signals that matter. They're the call pulling you toward a life that expands you.

Everything Else

Noise That Pulls You Off Course

Endless scrolling.

Negative news.

Chasing likes.

Impulse shopping.

Gossip.

Useless drama.

Toxic relationships.

Comfort food instead of action.

Binge-watching nothing.

Soul-crushing routine.

Playing it safe forever.

Three Gut-Check Questions for Identifying Your Call

1. Does it light you up like a Christmas tree?
2. Does it scare you enough that you'd regret not trying?
3. If you deny this, will you always wonder "what if"?

If all three hit, you've found your call to adventure.

But if you haven't found your call yet, that's okay too. Sometimes the call whispers before it shouts.

Bring out your curious kid.

And ask a lot of questions.

I'll never forget the "J Philosophy" I learned while working out at Santa Monica Beach.

J was a super-fit guy in his sixties with piercing blue eyes. He was always smiling and always at the workout area, no matter what time of day I showed up.

I'd say hi, and we'd chat about the fun things in life. He'd be stretching or doing difficult workout maneuvers and say things like, "I want to be a gymnast when I grow up."

He had this kid-like energy I connected with, but he looked like a buff wrestler in his wise years.

The kind of kid who asked *why* seventeen times in a row until your parents pretended not to hear you. Or the one who used *what if* like it was *please* (I was both).

What do you want to be when you grow up?

Not what you should want.
Not what pays the bills.
Not what sounds impressive at dinner parties.

What secretly makes your heart beat faster when you think about it?

DIRECTOR'S COMMENTARY

Every great film has that one scene where the hero can't stay the same anymore. It's the spark that lights the fuse.

Don't wait for perfect timing. Catalysts aren't neat or convenient. They show up when you least expect them.

The stars will never align.

But here's the Director's secret: what looks like chaos in the moment often becomes your 'happy accident' in the final cut.

Lean into the discomfort.

Your catalyst moment is coming. The question is, will you recognize it when it arrives?

Remember that blank page from Beat 1? This is what happens when you write on it instead of stare at it—opportunities show up.

KEY TAKEAWAYS

- Your wake-up call won't be convenient. It'll be uncomfortable and urgent.
- The call that scares you is usually the one you need to answer.
- You've already separated yourself from 80% of people by showing up and doing the work.
- Attachment to outcome creates pressure; presence creates performance.

ACTION!

This is your moment to ask curious questions and find the catalyst that's calling your name.

Be detailed.
See it.
Feel it.
Make it real.

You know the drill. Finish your next card and add it to your previous beats on your Director's Board.

The call has arrived.
Will you answer?

BEAT 4—MY WAKE-UP CALL

The Call
What event, opportunity, or inner pull is asking me
to step forward *right now*?

____

____

Gut Check
Does it light me up? ☐ Yes ☐ No
Does it scare me enough to matter? ☐ Yes ☐ No
Will I regret not trying? ☐ Yes ☐ No

Resistance
What's actually holding me back?
(Fear. Money. Judgment. Timing.)

____

The Truth
If I ignore this, what does my life look like one year
from now?

____

____

BEAT 5

FACE YOUR F.U.D.

"Resistance cannot be seen, touched, heard, or smelled. But it can be felt."

—Steven Pressfield, *The War of Art*

If you know what to do, why aren't you doing it?

Why don't you leave the job you hate?
Why don't you ask her out?
Why don't you take that adventure?
Why don't you call the person you had a falling out with?
Why don't you step onto the stage?

Why don't you go all in?
Why don't you start?
Why don't you finish?
Why don't you make the call?

You act like a sheep when you are a lion.
You say no when saying yes would make you feel alive.
You say yes when saying no would save you.

You procrastinate when it drains your life force.
You scroll when you know it's dumbing you down.
You hold in stress when it's killing you.

Why do you do it?
The funny thing is, you probably already know the answer. But the *not-so-funny thing* is how much it's already taken from you.

F.U.D.—fear, uncertainty, and doubt—is your brain's ancient alarm system.

And we've all let this beast *run and ruin our lives* far too much.

It was designed to keep you safe in a cave, protecting you from saber-toothed tigers and tribal rejection.

In modern life, it fires at job interviews, creative risks, hard conversations, and harsh online comments. But these can't actually kill you.

The problem?

Your brain can't tell the difference between real danger and uncomfortable growth.

That's why awareness matters.

When you condition yourself to recognize false alarms—through repeated exposure and conscious reframing—you literally rewire your neurology through neuroplasticity, the brain's ability to change and build new connections.

You teach your brain:
This isn't life or death.
This is growth.

The good news? You're not alone.
The bad news? F.U.D. is relentless.

It deploys three Terminators to kill your dreams:

Loss Pain.
Process Pain.
Outcome Pain.

And if you don't destroy them first, they will find you.
That's what they do.
That's all they do.
They absolutely will not stop—*ever*—until your dreams are dead.

F.U.D. ON THE FILM SET

"You fired our cinematographer, and we're shooting in less than two weeks?"

My body froze. I stared at my cousin in the driver's seat, waiting for her to say she was joking. She wasn't.

"Yeah. So you'll have to shoot it yourself," she said with that mix of certainty and delusion only a first-time film director can have.

Oh shit.

Let's rewind.

Mid-2020, Los Angeles—daily life disrupted by a global health crisis, shutdowns, and nonstop news alerts.

My cousin hired me to write a controversial feature film with diabolical characters and a loose story I felt compelled to shape. After the script, she brought me on as producer to shoot a two-minute proof of concept.

Simple plan: a few days of filming, a $7,500 budget, a small crew, then pitch for real funding.

My role: writer-producer. Keep her near budget, gather the crew, and execute beautifully.

I tried my best to be a tight-ass producer, but the creative chaos went from two days to five and the budget ballooned beyond anything we'd planned.

Meanwhile, my lovely wife Karen and I were forced to move out of our Burbank apartment with no income, crashing in a friend's guest room.

My cousin didn't see eye to eye with my film mentor, a seasoned cinematographer who had worked on major Hollywood films. He taught me so much over the years, and I loved being able to hire him as a thank-you.

Now he was gone, and I couldn't stop it.

Next, my cousin handed me his job like it was no big deal. She trusted I could do it, but didn't grasp what she was asking.

And me? I was forgetting that my lies were my limits—and I was getting smacked by F.U.D.

Now I had to storyboard every shot, coordinate all departments, and source new film gear in one week.

I'm not sharing that for sympathy, but because it's a clear example of how the reactionary mind can turn new opportunity into unnecessary stress if we're not careful.

THE INTERNAL DEBATE

Fear: What if you fail in front of the crew and your mentor hears?

Uncertainty: What if you don't capture what she wants and all that money is wasted?

Doubt: You're not ready for this.

Two other voices squared off:

Voice #1: "Say no. Safe. No expectations. No disaster."
Voice #2: "This could be exciting. Hollywood crew, dream gear, a new challenge."

I've journaled since I was fifteen; it gave me real-time awareness. I could see the F.U.D. punch winding up.

I looked at my cousin, overwhelmed by conflict and budget chaos. Replacing a cinematographer within a week would be madness.

If I said no, the shoot would likely suck. And I'd never find out if I could have saved it.

If I said yes, at least we had a shot.

I took a breath.

"This is crazy," I said. "I'll do it."

THE EXECUTION

It was stressful. Really stressful.

We were filming in a warehouse when the location owner stormed onto set, screaming at the top of his lungs about how we were using the space. Same guy who'd earlier shown us the rooftop and said, "You can rig the actress from here." Now he's losing it in front of everyone—and we'd paid him $1,500!

But it was also really cool.

One night, shooting in a luxury loft, I rode a curved camera dolly gliding through a scene. Our lead actor was playing a sleep-deprived and desperate man, searching for documents to prove that a company was destroying his life.

It was cinematic.

I felt like I was on a Spielberg set.

My creativity was stretched beyond anything I'd done. The veteran crew guided me when I needed it and trusted me when I didn't.

Then I made one huge mistake.

We were shooting a slow-motion scene at 120 frames per second. I forgot to reset the camera back to normal. The footage came back nearly three times too dark, and the sound was completely out of sync.

When I watched it back after the shoot, my heart fell out of sync.

That mistake wasted a lot of money. I was pissed at myself and felt like an idiot.

The sad part? *It was my cousin's favorite scene.* I screwed it up and we couldn't reshoot it.

That failure became a priceless lesson: take a beat and always triple-check your frame rate before rolling.

In filmmaking, it saves the scene.
In life, it saves your sanity, especially when the pressure's on.

In the end, I'm glad I fought the good F.U.D.

THE OUTCOME

Most of the footage looked like a Hollywood movie with intentional camera moves, lighting, and craftsmanship.

Those five days stretched me beyond anything I'd done. I learned more about filmmaking, leadership, and myself than I had in years.

My cousin, directing for the first time, learned hard lessons about budgets, relationships, and how excitement can override proper protocol.

The investment wasn't wasted. We finished a stunning proof of concept. Everyone who saw it asked, "What movie is that from? Is it on Netflix?"

I stepped into a role I wasn't ready for.
I made mistakes.
And I proved F.U.D. wrong, not by being perfect, but by saying yes when I wanted to say no.

Here's why I'm sharing this:

You grow by showing up.

If you don't step into the unknown, push your limits, take the shot, and choose curiosity over fear, you'll never find out what you're made of.

And when you do?
It feels damn good to know.

F.U.D. will always show up when opportunity knocks.
That's guaranteed.

Your job isn't to eliminate it.
It's to recognize it, acknowledge it, and take action before it gets back up.

Make your decision.
Take your shot.
Find out what you're capable of.
Because on the other side of that F.U.D. punch, that's where you grow the most.

"You have to let it all go—fear, doubt,
and disbelief. Free your mind."

—Morpheus, *The Matrix*

FOCUS YOUR CAMERA

Your brain is like a camera. Whatever you focus on magnifies.

Some people's camera is locked on negative news, danger, worst-case scenarios. So that's what gets magnified.

Your camera needs to focus on growth, adventure, love, new experiences, and your dreams. Focus there, and you'll see those magnify.

Here's what you need to remember—you don't get to turn the camera off.

You don't get to say "I'll focus later." You are always focusing on something, consciously or unconsciously.

As Tony Robbins often says: where your focus goes, your story flows.

Your life path is a result of your focus. Not luck, not where you grew up, not your parents or the economy or the government. Your focus.

Two kids can grow up in the same abusive home. One shuts down and freezes in time while the other strives to live better.

The difference?
Different focus.

What you focus on shapes how you feel, the decisions you make, the actions you take, and how you live.

Focus takes energy. If you bleed your energy out to nonsense and distractions—mind-numbing internet videos, toxic people, external status, reality TV, your worst inner critic—you will be terminated.

Before every decision, ask:
What am I focusing on?
Does it serve me?

When people share their fears, remember this.
They're showing you their footage, not reality.

When opportunity knocks, do a little research.
Then focus on what you might gain, not what you might lose.

Direction follows focus.
Always.

DRIFTING OR DIRECTING

Drifting is like going to the beach.

You lay your towel down, drop your things, and run into the ocean. You're swimming, playing, having fun—and before you realize it, your stuff is so far down the shore you can barely see it.

You drifted.
Without even noticing.

The same thing happens in life.

Your goals.
Your relationships.

One day, you look up and realize the current carried you so far from what mattered that you can barely remember what you were aiming for.

I learned this metaphor from Dean Graziosi, an exceptional teacher and partner of Tony Robbins.

I obsessed over it for weeks.

It became foundational to this book because drifting is one of life's most gradual killers.

And here's the undeniable truth:

Your life right now is the result of what you've put up with.
What you've settled for.

Who's in your life.
Who's not.
The joy or the pain you feel.
Your body.
Your love life.

How far you drifted.

It's all the product of what you tolerate.
And it all comes from these psychotic, relentless terminators.

Stop tolerating so much.

Fears, uncertainties, doubts, excuses, and distractions all drain you.

Whenever you put up with meaningless things that don't matter, you bleed out your energy, waste your time, and end up wondering what life you could have lived.

And the fact is, you don't have the time to waste.
No one does.

You might think, "Oh, I can always do that later." I'm telling you, no, you can't. Your life can be taken away in an instant, and you'll miss the opportunity.

When was the last time someone convinced you to abandon something you were excited about?

Maybe it was a career change, a creative project, a relationship, an adventure you wanted to take.

How did it feel when you listened to their fears instead of your dreams?

Where did that choice actually leave you? Are you living the life you designed... or the life someone else thought was "best for you"?

And what's even worse than that?
When you talk yourself out of it.

Let that hit you in your heart.

THE THREE TERMINATORS

Now that you understand how to focus your camera and avoid drifting, here's what you're actually up against.

F.U.D. doesn't show up as vague anxiety. It works through three specific pain patterns designed to keep you stuck:

Terminator 1: Loss Pain

What you think you'll lose by moving forward.

Like a hoarder clinging to broken furniture and boxes of junk, terrified to let go because deep down they believe their identity, their safety, their worth is tied up in all that clutter.

Real-world example: You cling to the job title that's killing you, the relationship that's draining you, the habits that are breaking you—because letting go feels like losing significance.

That "significance" is nothing but dead weight. And until you cut it, you'll never make space for what actually matters.

What dead weight are you clinging to?

Terminator 2: Process Pain

How much agony you'll be in during the journey.

Like staring at a mountain from the base, convinced the climb will destroy you, so you never take the first step.

Real-world example: You avoid starting the business because you imagine years of exhausting 80-hour weeks, when the reality is you'd find flow, excitement, and energy you never knew you had.

What journey are you avoiding because you've already decided it will be too painful?

Terminator 3: Outcome Pain

Where you will or will not end up.

Like a director so afraid their film will flop that they never yell "Action"—guaranteeing the only outcome is regret.

Real-world example: You don't ask her out because you're already living in the imagined future where she says no and you feel humiliated, missing the actual future where she says yes and changes your life.

What future are you afraid of that's keeping you from trying?

You need to recognize these terminators before they kill your dreams because here's the wild part: research confirms that people actually WANT this radical, cutting-edge thing called *life satisfaction*.

DIRECTOR'S NOTE:

I know. This is a lot.

You don't have to master it today. This chapter is your field manual. Come back when F.U.D. shows up (it will).

These aren't assignments—they're tools.

For now, identify which Terminator is hunting you and take one action this week to prove it wrong.

That's enough.

THE YELLOW HAT VS. THE BLACK HAT

Growing up, my mom had this saying: "The biggest risk in life is not taking one."

She was what Edward de Bono—psychologist and pioneer of creative thinking—called the "yellow hat" thinker: the optimist who always saw possibility. My dad? He wore the black hat. He often considered negative outcomes, worst-case scenarios, and reasons things wouldn't work

Both perspectives have value. My mom's optimism taught me to see opportunities. My dad's caution taught me to assess risks.

If you only wear the black hat, you never move.
If you only wear the yellow hat, you make reckless choices.
You need both.

That's the balance you're looking for in this beat: acknowledge the F.U.D., then move forward anyway, eyes wide open.

THE 40-70 RULE

Colin Powell—four-star general who made life-or-death decisions under pressure—had a rule: gather 40–70% of the information, then decide.

Less than 40%?
You're flying blind. Gambling, not deciding.

More than 70%?
The decision may have already been forced on you, or you've wasted the opportunity.

The film industry operates like a creative military requires calculated risks, not reckless gambles. You gather intel, assess, then call "Action" before the moment passes.

Here's how to use it:

- Gather 40–70% of the information
- Decide
- Learn from the feedback
- Adjust
- Repeat

Every action you take—win or lose—gives you data you didn't have before.

F.U.D. wants you to research forever. Information without action is sophisticated procrastination.

Don't enter the analysis paralysis forest because most who do never find their way out.

Take your shot. The camera's rolling.

MAKE YOUR OWN FILM

Stop comparing your rough cut to someone else's final cut, or you'll lose every time.

When you worry about what others think of you—*which is none of your business*—you hand the edit bay to an imaginary critic who doesn't care about your story.

The moment you compare your Scene 2 to someone else's Act III, you stop directing and start judging.

Progress stops.
Perfectionism begins.
And perfection is a myth invented by people who never finished making their movie.

Perfection-seeking keeps you stuck reshooting the same scene.

No distribution.

No premiere.

So what happens next?

You consider quitting.

Then you numb out—scrolling, binging, distracting yourself with life-sucking time wasters.

It's a brutal way to live.

But today, that cut ends.

Here's the only comparison that matters:

Your last take.

Your last scene.

Your last year.

Make it better than *that*.

Stop trying to star in someone else's movie.

Start directing your own.

DIRECTOR'S COMMENTARY

It's Your Life.

Right now, there's something you want to do.
Something that excites you.
Something that matters to YOU.

And then there's that person—maybe someone who loves you—telling you to wait. To be practical. To play it safe.
Is someone else pulling your focus?
It has to be you. What are you going to focus on?

Your decisions direct your life.
But the way you make better decisions comes directly from your state of being.

People try to make their dreams happen from a slumped low-energy state while they compare themselves to celebrities who are in their own lane. And they wonder why they don't make progress.

Stop.

Get into a beautiful state of being first:

Take a cold shower
Talk to a happy friend
Play with your dog (or show up at a dog park with a tennis ball)
Take a walk without your phone.
Be present.

Then, make one decision that's completely yours.

Stop letting meaningless nothings run your life.
Stop running someone else's projector.
Focus your camera on what you can control.

Stop drifting.

Because if you don't direct your life, someone else will.
And their movie won't be nearly as satisfying as yours.

KEY TAKEAWAYS

- F.U.D. is your brain's ancient alarm system. Recognize it, don't obey it.
- Focus your camera on growth, not fear. Direction follows focus.
- The Three Terminators that hunt you: Loss Pain, Process Pain, Outcome Pain.
- 40-70% information is enough. Decide and move.
- Stop editing someone else's movie. Progress beats perfection.

ACTION!

Time to face your F.U.D. head-on and design your response system.

If you have a red pen, use it.
This is where fear gets exposed.

Move fast.
Be honest.

This isn't analysis.
It's confrontation.

When you're done filling out your next card, get it on your Director's Board.

Your F.U.D. isn't going anywhere.
But now you know how to recognize it, refocus, and take your shot anyway.

The debate is over.
You've made the decision.
We gotta roll.

BEAT 5—MY F.U.D.

The Avoidance
What decision am I avoiding right now because of fear, uncertainty, or doubt?

____
____

The Dominant Fear
Which is stopping me most?
□ Loss Pain □ Process Pain □ Outcome Pain

Reality Check
What's the worst that could actually happen if I act?
(Be specific—not catastrophic.)

____
____

New Commitment
"Despite my F.U.D. telling me _____________
I'm taking action on _____________ this week."

ACT II
BUiLD YOUR
CAST & CREW

"No mind is complete by itself. It needs contact and association with other minds to grow and expand."

—Napoleon Hill, *Think and Grow Rich*

BEAT 6

ALL iN

"The biggest risk in life is not taking one."

—Mom

When you fully commit, you have no idea where it might lead.

In 2017, my dad—a working actor—got the call. He'd booked a one-day shoot on a major film, *The Irishman*, directed by one of my all-time favorites, Martin Scorsese.

The scene?
A mobster warns my dad about his "wild son."

First thought: I could play the wild son!
Second thought: Even if I just get on that set to observe, I'll learn for life.

So I asked, "Dad, can I come with you to set?"

My dad, with his full Italian-Jersey accent, replied:

"Tone, I haven't worked with these guys since *Casino.* It's a one-day shoot in New York. I can't ask for favors."

I was disappointed but not defeated.

I asked myself: *What if I went anyway?*

What if I flew to New York and figured out how to get on set when I got there?

Then came the dilemma: I was supposed to fly back to the Philippines to see Karen—the girl I'd fallen in love with during my extended vacation. I'd planned to propose.

But the dates clashed.

Love or career?
Comfort or calling?

The stakes were high. If I failed, I'd be out thousands of dollars I didn't have. I'd disappoint Karen, who'd been waiting for me. And what if I actually got on set…and nothing came from it?

Fear, uncertainty, and doubt crept in like a thick fog.

That's when I did what every smart Director does when the shoot gets complicated.

I called in my crew.

When you're at a crossroads, mindset is everything. I could've easily sunk into a fixed mindset and let F.U.D. win—telling myself it wasn't worth the risk, that it was better to stay safe and stick to my original plans.

Instead, I gathered friends and family who supported me: Chad, Shane, Cyrus, and my sister. We met at a pizza place.

"I'm thinking of crashing the set in New York, but I'm not invited and I don't have money to schlep around searching. Is that insane?"

They backed me instantly.
They reminded me of what I already knew deep down.
This opportunity might never come again.

I booked the ticket—on credit—and prepared to act before I felt ready.

A few nights later, I met up with Chad again. We came up with this brilliant idea: print my acting headshots and find the casting director for the film.

Because, you know, they'd see me and say, "Cool, you have no real film credits, wanna be in the movie?"

I didn't have a plan.
Just a feeling.

At a red light, Chad turned, looked me dead in the eyes, and yelled:

"You're going to be in this movie! You're going to be in this movie! You're going to be in this movie!"

He said it like it was real. He yelled it with such certainty and passion that it hit me like a punch in the chest.

I got chills.

Tony Robbins calls it an *incantation*—a full-body belief statement.

That shout shattered my doubt. It was the opposite of F.U.D.
It was raw certainty.

I flew to New York the next day, powered by that belief.

NO TURNING BACK

I was in New York.
I was running out of time and money.

I walked the streets, trying to find the casting director.
I couldn't.

I eventually found their number and called.
After my nervous rambling, they mistook me for my dad.
They assumed I was calling to thank them.
Then they said they would get back in touch.

I was getting discouraged.
But I didn't stop.

I had one contact—Gary.
An assistant to one of the actors in the film.
A friend.

I called him.
I told him my situation.
He said he'd ask around and see what he could do.

That was the turning point.
I suppressed my ego and asked directly for help.

I finally called my dad.
He was already nearby in New Jersey, staying with my grandma, prepping for the shoot. I told him I'd randomly decided to visit and made my way over.

The moment I arrived, everything shifted.

My dad's first words were:
"Hey, did you talk to anyone? I got a message from production. They said, 'Hey Phil, your son Tony is welcome to come on set.'"

And just like that, my whole face turned into a smile of relief and gratitude.

I felt the power of networking.
Opportunities happen through relationships, not résumés.
One genuine connection can open doors you didn't know existed.

"Life, uh... finds a way."

—Dr. Ian Malcolm, *Jurassic Park*

THE SHOOT—DAY

The next morning, I walked on set beside my dad.

I wore my grandma's fur coat.
Chad said I would stand out.
Plus it was cold outside.

He was on a roll so far.
I didn't question him.

First, Dad and I were shown to his trailer.

DAD

Hey Tone, listen, if you're on set, don't get in my
eyeline, okay? It's been a while, ya know?

TONY

(holding in a laugh)

Of course. I'll be a fly on the wall.
This is gonna be awesome!

Then a fun-loving executive producer named Jai escorted me to set.

I was nearly bursting with excitement.

I saw Joe Pesci, Robert De Niro, and Martin Scorsese discussing the scene
next to a beautiful 1970s Chevrolet El Camino.

I stood there, arms crossed, watching these legends work, and I thought:

What if I didn't fly to New York?
What if I gave up before?
What if I turned back when things seemed too hard?

That thought alone makes the decision to act so important.

Then Joe Pesci said something to Martin Scorsese.
They both looked over at me, then back at each other.
Pesci gave him a quick Italian hug.
Scorsese walked away.

Huh, that was weird.

And then the wildest thing happened.
Pesci called me over.

PESCI

Tony, come 'ere.

I walk over with a huge, confused gr*in. (My dad and Joe had worked together before—I grew up around him. That's how he knew my name.)*

TONY

(playing it cool)

Hey Joe, how you doin'?

PESCI

You're gonna be in this scene. No lines, but you'll be in it with me and De Niro. Can you handle that?

TONY

Really? Yeah, I'm ready. I'd love to. Thank you!

PESCI

But don't fuck this up, or I'll smack you in the
head, okay? I'm serious.

TONY

(giddy but scared)

Yeah, I know you're serious. I'm ready.

My heart raced as he introduced me to one of my favorite directors, Martin
Scorsese, and suddenly I was cast as *The Wild Son!*

SCORSESE

(speaking fast)

Hey, nice to meet ya. I like the hair, you got the
look.

TONY

Thank you.

SCORSESE

Okay, you're gonna play The Wild Son.

Can you be wild?

TONY

Wild's my middle name!

SCORSESE

(pointing at me)

But not too wild... Okay, great. Let's get you to
hair and makeup.

An hour later, I had a new slicked-back mobster haircut and was sent straight to De Niro's trailer—which, to my surprise, felt like a meditation zone, with relaxing music and incense.

DE NIRO

Hey, how you doin'? Can we put a tattoo on your
arm?

TONY

(on cloud nine)

Yeah, whatever you need.

About an hour later, I was back on the film set. I stood behind a jewelry counter. De Niro on my left. Pesci and my dad two feet away from me. Two massive film cameras and a full crew.

Before we rolled, Pesci gave me some ideas about my character. Then De Niro walked up to me, eyeing my hair.

DE NIRO

Can we cut your sideburns higher? In the '70s
gangsters had 'em higher.

TONY

Yeah, do whatever you need.

De Niro turned to the on-set hairstylist. He grabbed her clippers and—with the precision of a seasoned barber—buzzed my sideburns up to the exact spot he thought was right.

De Niro gave me a haircut.

The scene started with Pesci badmouthing me to my dad.

He warned him.

Then he and De Niro left.

Moments later—*now directly in my dad's eyeline*—my own father walked up to me and smacked me in the head.

DAD

What's the matter with you, huh?

This was one of those do-or-die moments.

Having no line, I could've stayed silent and reacted. But my dad always told me: If you're on set and a principal actor says something to you, and it makes sense, you can say something back. You might get a pay bump. Your line might even make it in the film.

TONY

What?

A series of takes followed. I improvised some more. I even dropped a curse word or two.

SCORSESE

And cut! Tony, I liked what you said the first time.
Let's do another like that.

Ultimately, my scene *and my line*, "What?," stayed in the film. Around minute 40, if you're wondering.

There was nothing like being at the world premiere in 2019.
Seeing myself on the big screen with my film heroes.
Hearing the entire theater laugh out loud when I got smacked in the head.

Pesci really foreshadowed that.

THE REALITY ABOUT CONNECTIONS

Here's the irony: *Joe Pesci is my godfather. He baptized me. Literally.*

Yes, the Academy Award–winning actor—a.k.a. the deadliest film gangster in history.

So why didn't I ask him for *an offer I couldn't refuse* in the first place?

Joe didn't even know I was coming to set. The guy changes his phone number more than most people change their socks.

I learned long ago not to expect family favors in Hollywood. More importantly, that's not how life works.

You don't wait around for favors.
You take action.
You show up.

You position yourself to receive help.

Even when you have connections, you still have to prove you're serious. I had to take the risk, spend the money, fly to New York, and get myself on set through my own effort. Only then was I positioned for Joe to help.

The connection didn't replace the courage—it amplified it. The string Pesci pulled for me is one I'll never forget. It was one of the best gifts of my life.

This beat taught me that transformation never happens alone—it's always *We*, not *Me*.

F.U.D. had done its job. It made me pause and consider the risks. But I didn't let it make my decision.

I've learned that the fastest way to "figure it out" is to step forward, ready or not.

Turns out I was onto something.

When you take action despite incomplete information you are more likely to achieve breakthrough opportunities than those who wait for "perfect" conditions.

Don't get lost in analysis paralysis.
Go for it.

THE DECISION TO ACT

Here's the note to my younger self that you need to read: the most important skill to develop is communication and networking. Period. Go do that before anything else.

Make your decisions fast and change them slow. Go with your gut.

Remember the 40–70 Rule from Beat 5? When you have 40–70% of the information, decide. More data won't eliminate risk—it delays action.

I knew if I didn't take the trip, I'd regret it, whichever way it went. I already felt the years slipping by without making moves, wishing instead of acting.

I didn't try to get every part of the plan together—just enough. Then I decided to go for it. I bought the ticket and cut everything else off.

Don't wait until everything is perfectly lined up to make your move because that will never happen. Learn to trust your gut.

That one-day scene changed everything, but the bigger transformation wasn't landing in the movie. It was realizing it would have never happened if I didn't decide to go all in, cut everything else off, and follow through.

DIRECTOR'S COMMENTARY

Jump through that window of opportunity before it slams shut.

If this sounds harder than the earlier beats, that's normal. There comes a moment when you need to stop analyzing the script and actually walk on set. It's not perfect. You're not totally ready. But you put on that fur coat and step forward anyway.

Confidence isn't a prerequisite—it's a by-product. The action comes first. The confidence shows up after you begin.

Your old script can't follow you into this next act. The patterns you've outgrown will try to cling to you, but you have to leave them behind if you want a new story.

And that resistance you feel—the voice whispering "you're not ready"? That's the exact cue that you are.

Resistance isn't a stop sign; it's an indicator that you're pointed in the right direction.

When in doubt, ask your future self. Imagine the version of you who already made the leap. What would your most courageous, decisive self tell you right now?

And don't discount your crew. Sometimes belief comes from within. Other times, it takes a friend yelling in your ear—someone who sees your potential before you see it yourself.

Position yourself so help can actually reach you. Even with connections, you still have to show up first.

Networks amplify courage—they don't replace it.

KEY TAKEAWAYS

- Decide at 40–70% of the information, then go ALL IN.
- Proximity is power—put yourself where opportunity lives.
- A strong belief can destroy doubt.
- Fighting and overcoming *the resistance* is always worth it.

ACTION!

You're done debating.
Time to make decisions fast and from the gut.

You're leaving the old ordinary world for the new one.
You're crossing your threshold.

This is where hesitation ends and your real story begins.

Create your next card.
Look at it.
Read it aloud.

This is the moment your story shifts.

Progress never happens solo, but the decision to move forward always starts with you.

My dad opened the door. Chad gave me conviction. Gary made calls. Pesci pulled one unforgettable string for me—a gift I'll never forget.

But none of that mattered until I chose to go all in.

Every hero who crosses the threshold discovers the same truth: action is the gateway. Allies show up *after* you move.

Take a breath. You've committed.
Here we go.
Pictures up.

BEAT 6—ALL IN

The Decision
What new way of thinking am I choosing—and what am I going *all in* on?

A Declaration
From my future self—the version of me who went all in. What would they tell me with no hesitation?

Commitment Check
What has to happen—starting today—for me to follow through on this decision?

BEAT 7

CONNECTiNG THE DOTS

"You can't connect the dots looking forward; you can only connect them looking backwards. So you have to trust that the dots will somehow connect in your future."

—Steve Jobs

I sat on the rooftop of my Santa Monica office at midnight, feeling something I'd never felt before: free.

Three years earlier, I couldn't make eye contact with a barista without rehearsing my coffee order.

I avoided dating.
I never initiated.
I waited to be chosen and stayed invisible.

Now? I act before I overthink. Like when I saw an attractive girl at a bus stop—I walked up, smiled, held out my phone with "Add Contact" open, and she entered her number without me saying a word.

I wasn't trying to be clever.
I was deliberately doing things the old version of me believed were impossible. I was gathering evidence instead of hiding.

B STORY

In screenwriting, the B Story is the subplot that runs parallel to your main plot—typically a relationship or supporting character who teaches the hero what they need to learn.

While the A Story is about external goals (getting the job, winning the fight, solving the case), the B Story is about internal transformation. It's your mentor who believes in you when you don't believe in yourself. Your best friend who challenges your bullshit. The environment that forces you to evolve.

In *The Lord of the Rings*, Frodo's A Story is destroying the ring. His B Story is the fellowship—Sam, Gandalf, Aragorn—the people who carry him when he can't carry himself.

In your life, your B Story is the supporting cast and environments that shape who you become when you're not looking.

Beat 6 was about the decision to act. Beat 7 is about the ecosystem that sustains your transformation.

You can make all the bold moves you want, but if you return to toxic environments with energy vampires, you'll slide back to your old self.

The Nomad Years

For a chunk of my adult life, I moved constantly: warehouse, sister's garage gym, friend's couch, back to my dad's place, tiny studio, secret office, and more addresses than I care to count.

I once romanticized that nomadic lifestyle, convincing myself constant motion meant freedom. In reality, it left me inconsistent, exhausted, and broke more often than not. I wasn't exploring—I was drifting. An observer moving from one backdrop to the next.

But slowly and steadily, I course-corrected year by year.
Each move changed where I slept and who I became.

The Seedy Warehouse

After college, crashing in my dad's converted garage, I found a Craigslist ad that would redirect my life:

"Creative commune. Free food and board in exchange for work directing calls and filming a weekly LIVE talk show with sex therapist Dr. Suzy Block."

It was a sketchy downtown L.A. warehouse that felt more like a Tarantino film set than a housing ad. But I needed to move out. Nothing screamed louder than that wild post. How could I not go check it out?

Max, Dr. Suzy's husband, handed me a key and a philosophy: "Live free. Stay curious."

My time there gave me dozens of journal entries—it felt like a documentary about *odd human outcasts in the wild*. I almost fit right in.

I had my own space, worked only four hours a day answering phones and filming a weekly talk show that would make Howard Stern blush.

Yes, it was strange. And yes, I saw more than I wanted to. But there was a liberation in being separated from the mainstream world and observing the underground.

I spent most of my time mastering DIY filmmaking and creating ridiculous YouTube skits with my friends.

The warehouse taught me radical open-mindedness. When you're surrounded by people living completely different lives than you ever imagined, you stop judging and start observing.
That curiosity became my superpower.

After eleven months, it was time to move on.

I moved into my sister's garage gym.
It gave me time to recalibrate and *reflect*.

Literally—my bed was surrounded by workout gear, vintage bodybuilder photos, and full-wall mirrors.

I'd see myself in ways a man shouldn't.

That's where I created a spec commercial for a healthy drink company. I shot it on my own dime, hoping they'd buy it.

Over a hundred entries, they picked mine!

$7,500.
My first real directing paycheck.

It was a true turning point.
One I was proud of.

Six months later, it was time to move on *again*.

Onto a friend's couch, always one step ahead of broke, waiting for that check.

The Motorcycle Mentor

The payment was delayed for months.

A copyright issue with the music I'd used threw the project into legal limbo. Out of money, I posted my motorcycle for sale on Craigslist.

A tall French guy named Sacha showed up.

"This thing could be in a movie," he said, running his hand over the frame.

"I know," I replied. "I really don't want to sell it...by the way, what do you do?"

"I'm a cameraman in the film industry."

He never bought the bike, but he hired me at his film company, became my mentor, and eventually shot multiple projects with me.

That didn't happen through LinkedIn requests or "Can I pick your brain?" emails. It happened through genuine connection when I wasn't trying to get anything.

Even though I was desperate, I remained friendly and open-minded. You meet people differently that way. No agenda. Just authentic presence.

That's when mentorship happens.

Sacha became part of my fellowship—someone who believed in my vision when I was starting out.

The Secret Office

I found salvation above a liquor store in Santa Monica.

I convinced the owner to rent me an office for $400 a month. But he didn't know that office was about to become my secret home for nearly four years.

I wanted to live near the beach among people playing a bigger game than me. On my budget, that required creativity.

Creativity came with trade-offs.

This was covert living.
A daily con.

Every morning before leaving, I had to make the space look like a functioning business office in case the landlord—who owned the store below and was constantly up and down the stairs—glanced through the door. Or worse, if he walked in.

It was an L-shaped office wedged above a liquor store, the ugly duckling of the building's five units. No kitchen. No shower. So I'd hit the YMCA around the corner for workouts and hot water.

I constructed a DIY Murphy wall bed that transformed my sleeping quarters into a workspace by day and a creative studio by night. Papers scattered just right. A coffee mug strategically placed. The performance of productivity.

But it was across from a gorgeous park, near Whole Foods Market, and only a twelve-minute bike ride to the beach.

That tiny office became my gateway to adulthood as an artist. For the first time in my life, I had a place that was mine. On my terms. No roommates. No family watching. Just me, my ambitions, and the blank page.

Low rent bought freedom. Freedom created space. Space allowed transformation.

I finally had the margin to invest in myself properly.

I found a therapist. She worked with me every week for nearly two years—not because I was broken, but because I was tired of carrying baggage from a past relationship where I'd lost a girlfriend to PTSD.

I'd spent two years as a caretaker instead of a partner, watching someone I loved struggle with demons I couldn't fight for her. When it ended, I lost the relationship and my sense of self.

Therapy helped me untangle who I was from who I thought I needed to be for someone else. It gave me permission to set boundaries. To recognize that loving someone doesn't mean drowning with them. To understand that I could be a good person without sacrificing my own mental health.

The secret office became my implementation hub. It was where I studied personal development, practiced new habits, and rebuilt my identity from the ground up.

But I still needed one more piece: connection.

The Jacuzzi Connection

The YMCA became my second home—strength training, hot showers, and the jacuzzi. When you're living above a liquor store with no hot water, chlorine-soaked relaxation feels like a resort.

One day, a random guy struck up a conversation in the steam.

Turns out we were both magicians—rare in the wild. His name was Chad.

We started meeting regularly and not just for magic tricks. For life design. We both had whiteboards covering our walls, mapping goals and dreams. He was naturally social; I was the observer.

Watching him interact with strangers felt like watching a muscle I hadn't trained yet.

We became accountability partners.
He helped me break out of my shell, and I helped him prioritize his ambitions. We amplified each other's confidence.
He was the guy who would later yell, "You're going to be in this movie!" when I needed it most (Beat 6).

But more than that, he became proof that friendships could be built on mutual growth instead of mutual dysfunction.

The best relationships happen when you show up as equals, genuinely curious about each other's worlds. Support flows both ways.

All that practice showing up—with Chad, mentors, and new spaces—started bleeding into everyday life and connecting the dots.

The Experiment

Becoming a scientist at heart changed the way I moved through the world.

I was visiting New York, staying in Manhattan. Walking by a Thai restaurant, I turned in slow motion and saw this beautiful Thai girl working as the hostess. I paused—probably too long—taken in by her beauty.

Then I walked forward about ten feet before stopping again, leaning against a lamp post. For fifteen minutes, my mind went back and forth:

Maybe I could talk to her.
Maybe I could ask her about Thailand since I had a trip coming up.
What if she thinks I'm weird?

What if...

I passed by one more time, telling myself I'd go in and talk to her. What did I do?

Walked into the restaurant, asked her what time they closed, and went back to my apartment alone and defeated.

What time do you close?
Idiot.

After thirty minutes of beating myself up, I finally snapped.

"No. I'm going to do an experiment. Like I'm a scientist. It doesn't matter if I fail. It doesn't matter if I succeed. I want to see what happens if I actually go in there and have a conversation with her."

To some, this might sound like high-school nerves, but that's the thing about a disempowering identity—it traps you in what seems simple or effortless to others.

And if you're a hopeless romantic, you get it. When someone truly sparks something in you, your whole system glitches. Confidence short-circuits. Logic disappears. It takes a little rewiring to function again.

So I reframed it.

This wasn't about impressing her.
This wasn't about "winning."
This was an experiment to override fear and see what happened on the other side.

I went back down there, walked in, asked a couple questions, and casually mentioned I was going to Thailand.

Then I surprised myself:

"Would you want to grab tea sometime and tell me what to expect?"

She said yes.

I was mentally skipping all the way back to my Airbnb.

We spent the next three days together. She brought me to an underground Thai dance club. I performed magic for her friends. It was Halloween, so we went to a costume contest party. It was pure fun.

The experiment was a success, not because we had a beautiful time, but because I took action to see what would happen.

I got curious, stayed playful, and stopped overthinking.

If you adopt this experimental mindset whenever you're stuck in your head, life gets lighter.

When in doubt, start playing scientist.

"Happiness is only real when shared."

—Christopher McCandless, *Into the Wild*

After moving *way too many times* in a short period, I started noticing something undeniable: your environment shapes you far more than most people realize.

Harvard psychologist Dr. Brian Little's research shows that while we have stable traits, who we become in practice is heavily influenced by context, environment, and the personal projects we commit to.

When you change your surroundings, it's easier to change your habits.

My secret office was proof.

Minimal rent meant freedom.
Freedom created space.
Space allowed expansion.
Expansion led to transformation.

Every environment I chose—or avoided—shaped me.

And the other half?
Every person I met—or didn't—shaped me too.

- The warehouse helped me become radically open-minded
- The YMCA people forced me to become social
- Sacha showed me that mentorship emerges through authentic connection

This is the real work of your B Story—connect the dots as you move through it because it's the only way your A Story ever comes together.

DIRECTOR'S COMMENTARY

The people and places in our lives make us or break us. If you don't understand that, you will be lost—however smart you are.

Ask better questions.

Are you stuck in environments that don't serve the person you're trying to become, or are you staying comfortable in spaces that keep you small? Who are your mentors—and are they still helping you grow? Are your friends challenging you or simply comforting you? Do your spaces fuel creativity and growth, or quietly drain it?

This is where most people slow down. But if you keep it steady, it's where the real shift begins. Nurture your B Story.

KEY TAKEAWAYS

- Stay away from energy vampires.
- Mentorship happens through authentic connection, not transactional requests.
- Environment shapes identity—change your surroundings to change yourself.
- Sometimes adventurous distractions keep you sane—they're pressure valves, not failures.

ACTION!

Everything you've gone through—and everyone you've met—has meaning.
But meaning isn't automatic.
It's assigned.

This is where you decide what those people and places mean going forward—and who they're helping you become.

Time to recalibrate the relationships and environments shaping your identity.

Time to connect the dots.

Manifest your connection:
One environment you're changing
One mentor or peer you're seeking out
One new place you'll explore this week
One energy vampire—person, place, habit, or digital drain—you need to put a stake in

Fill out your next card and pin it beside the others on your Director's Board.

You've taken the call.
You've shown up.
You're building your support system.

Your fellowship is forming.

BEAT 7—MY CONNECTION

Connecting The Dots
Where do I spend most of my time—and how do those people and places shape my energy, creativity, and confidence?

____

____

The Circle
The five people I interact with most.
Next to each, mark whether they lift or drain me.

__________ ↑ / ↓
__________ ↑ / ↓
__________ ↑ / ↓
__________ ↑ / ↓
__________ ↑ / ↓

The Gap
What kind of mentor would serve my next chapter?
Business · Creative · Personal · Spiritual · Relationship

BEAT 8
EXPAND YOUR BEiNG

"Are we having fun yet?"

—Castor Troy, *Face/Off*

Ever feel like you've done everything "right,"
but your life still looks like it's a faded
black-and-white projector reel from the 1930s?

Where's the color?

The expansion?

The playful exploration of who you can actually become?

There's one contradiction that keeps you stuck: a cognitive dissonance most people can't snap out of.

The very thing you're scared of is the exact thing that will give you the life you want.

You're one decision away from shifting your story from a quiet rerun nobody asked for to a life worth watching and *rewatching*.

In filmmaking, these are the trailer moments—the scenes that make you lean forward in your seat:

- *The Matrix*: Neo realizing he can dodge bullets

- *Rocky*: The training montage

- *Spider-Man*: Peter Parker discovering his powers

They're not conflict-free.
There are stumbles, failures, and awkward first takes.

But they're exploration.
Discovery.
The joy of becoming someone new.

Beat 6 was about the decision to act.
Beat 7 was about building your environment and support system.

Beat 8 is where you step into your new world and discover who you're becoming.

Your life can have trailer moments.
Every day, week, month, and year.

But you'll need to edit them in.

Before we continue, I want you to imagine this next part the way I lived it—like text flashing across a movie trailer.

This is where the fun and games begin.
The expansion.
The experimentation.
A new identity taking shape.

The lights dim.

The tension rises.

And the story shifts...

THE TRAILER

HE MADE A CHOICE MOST PEOPLE SAVE FOR RETIREMENT

At 30, I booked a one-way ticket to the Philippines and lived in a beach house with nothing but ocean as my front yard.

Not because I was rich.
Because I refused to wait.

The moment I stepped off that plane, I discovered something profound: I could navigate a foreign country, handle whatever came up, and thrive in complete uncertainty.

But it started with a major concern.

Halfway to my destination, the taxi driver pulled over on an empty road and walked away. Fight-or-flight kicked in.

Was this a trap?
Was he going to pull me out of the car somewhere?
Was my dad right about going here?

I glanced in the rearview mirror...
I saw what he was doing.
I let out a laugh of relief.

He was peeing against a wall.

I already love this country.

First lesson learned:
Fear will tell you it's a threat.
Curiosity will show you it's just a guy peeing on the side of the road.

THE PHONE CALL THAT TRIED TO STOP HIM

The call came out of nowhere.

My dad's voice—thick Jersey accent, already suspicious.

"So uh… what'd you want to tell me?"

I took an excited *and reluctant* breath.

"Dad, I'm leaving for Asia. I'm starting in the Philippines."

Silence.

Then disbelief.

"The Philippines? Don't you watch the news? It's dangerous."

"Have you ever been there?" I asked, trying not to bicker.

"Well… no," he said. "But shouldn't you be working on your career? You could always go in ten years."

Ten years.

I let that number hang in the air.

Ten years from now, I'd be thirty-nine—my current age as I write this book.

Would I still have the energy and guts to backpack through remote islands?

Or would I be like him—comfortable, cautious, convinced the world was too dangerous?

If I waited ten years, I wouldn't be the same person who wanted to go. I'd be the person who wished he had.

The truth?
I was annoyed.
But I also expected it.

That's why he was the last person I told. And I'd already booked the ticket. Good thing, too. When parents say *wait*, something in us wants to move. Even as adults.

I wasn't going to miss my chance at personal freedom. *What if* is the slowest kind of regret.

Here's the irony: my dad is cool.

He was the courageous one in his family.
He left Jersey for Los Angeles to become an actor—what my grandma called "a place where a bunch of vagabonds lived."
He took his own leap into the unknown and made it.

I used to show my friends the mafia films he was in and ask them with a straight face,

"So… what does your dad do?"

But years of responsibility and TV programming dulled his adventurous spark.

I made an oath: never lose curiosity when I reach my wiser years.

Dad often wears the "Black Hat" from Edward de Bono's *Six Thinking Hats*— the perspective that asks what could go wrong. It's the cautious, critical voice that spots dangers and risks. I thank him for it. His protection plan tested whether my dreams were worth pursuing anyway.

And he gave me half the stories in this book.
Thanks, Dad.

Of course, I didn't fly into another country blind.

Months before my trip, I researched and immersed myself in Asia. I even hired a virtual assistant who lived there to help me navigate. I gathered about sixty percent of the information—right in that forty-to-seventy sweet spot—and followed my heart.

My dad probably thought I was crazy, but I was switching on adventure mode, trusting my gut, and going all in.

The payoff?
Now I carry a lifetime of stories and lessons that only exist because I refused to wait.

None of it would have happened if I'd waited ten years.

HE EXPANDED HIS MAP

This is the part your ego hates.
Suppress that little bastard.

In Neuro-Linguistic Programming (NLP)—the study of how language and thought patterns shape us—Richard Bandler teaches that we all carry a personal *map* of reality.

The problem?
Most maps are tiny, filled with limitations based on incomplete information.

Three map errors that keep you stuck:

- **Generalization:** "All foreign countries are dangerous."
- **Distortion:** "I'm not the type who can handle adventure."
- **Deletion:** "I can't afford to travel." (ignoring creative solutions)

I'd already expanded my map in my twenties—motorcycling solo across America, living in warehouses, crashing on couches. I wasn't starting from zero. But the Philippines? That would stretch my map in ways I couldn't predict.

Research in neuroscience shows that new experiences and unfamiliar places stimulate neuroplasticity—the brain's ability to form new neural connections—and are associated with heightened creativity and cognitive flexibility that can persist well beyond the experience itself.

Go somewhere new, become someone new.

No wonder I came back with new confidence, another feature film script written, conversational Filipino language skills, and a gorgeous wife who somehow still tolerates what I call *animated eloquence*—which is a euphemism for saying I'm an energy ball.

If you're reading this, KareBear: gihigugma tika. And in case I did something stupid recently—I'm sorry, forgive me, thank you, I love you.

THE BAMBOO TELEGRAM WAS SENT

Living in Santander, Philippines, taught me a different kind of fame: word of mouth. Within days, everyone knew there was a young American living in the beach house.

I'd ride my dirt bike deep into backroads and hear my name shouted from porches—not because they were shunning me, but because I'd become part of that little town.

Several times, girls would zip past us on scooters, giggling, "Hi, Tony!" It was surreal—like Tom Cruise without the entourage.

Karen—my girlfriend then, now my wife—probably wondered if I'd play island Casanova.

I didn't.

Though the island had its playful humor. Some stories stay between us.

One of my favorite moments?

When I performed magic for Karen's barangay—her neighborhood. I showed up with cards and coins and even turned a ₱100 peso note into a US dollar. The look on her uncle Tino's face was priceless. Suddenly I had a crowd of curious kids and amazed adults.

For a shy kid who used to mumble through life, this was proof.

When you show up authentically, the world makes room for you.

HE CHOSE RESILIENCE OVER RERUNS

It wasn't all paradise.

One evening, while riding my motorcycle in flip-flops, I was bitten by something venomous.

My ankles swelled like balloons.
Hours passed.
The pain wouldn't stop.

The nearest real hospital?
A five-hour bus ride or a 45-minute ferry to another island. But it was night.
The last ferry had already left!

After a sleepless night watching my ankles swell, 5 a.m. finally arrived. I hobbled onto my motorcycle with Karen on back, limped onto the ferry, rode to the city, and found a private hospital.

Diagnosed.
Treated.
Relieved.

The best part?
The doctor visit was only $40.
Back in the States, that consultation would've cost three times as much.

At those prices, I almost got a prostate check just for fun.

Old map: "Third world hospitals could be the end of me."

New map: "Adventures demand resilience. Filipino doctors are top-notch."

HE FOUND JOY IN THE MUNDANE

Karen wanted to stop at 7-Eleven, and I gave her the universal "Do we have to?" face. In America, 7-Eleven means fluorescent lighting, questionable hot dogs, and a hoodlum or two loitering by the door.

The Philippines version?
It's a cool hangout spot.
They've got tables and chairs out front with friendly people.

Inside, we walked down an aisle when a song played on the radio, and she started singing along.

Then, on the next aisle, another customer joined in.
Then a woman mopping the floor.
Then, when we went to pay, the cashier—you guessed it—he was singing while ringing us up.

My face hurt from smiling.
It was like a Disney movie.

No one planned it.
No one was embarrassed.
They were joyful.

Moments like that, I'll never forget—you can't script those.
You can only be present enough to notice them.

Old map: "Convenience stores are depressing—get in, get out, don't make eye contact."

New map: "Anywhere becomes an adventure when you're present enough to enjoy it."

FROM STRANGERS TO STORIES

A German adventurer who'd biked across Asia and lived with headhunters tossed me a helmet.

"Hop on the dirt bike."

This was Karlheinz—Karl.
Indiana Jones if Indiana wore flip-flops.

We raced through the busy city, dodging potholes and people, until we got a flat tire in a sketchy alley.

In L.A., alleys aren't the safest places.
But in the Philippines, I learned a lot about *alleys*.

While Karl spoke Filipino with a local, I peered deeper into the alley and spotted a shirtless man singing karaoke against a wall, Buddha belly and all. No audience. Just a man having fun with a song.

You better believe I took out my camera and filmed it.

Karl was in his seventies when I met him—yet he lived with more vitality, curiosity, and humor than most twenty-year-olds. He owned businesses in Germany and the Philippines, took me deep into the mountains to his farm, and showed me what a life of presence actually looks like.

Around him, adventure wasn't an event.
It was a mindset.

Joy isn't something you find. It's something you carry.

Karl taught me that, and I've tried to carry it ever since.

This is the important part:

It's your job—and mine—to bring your best self to whatever situation you're in.

Whether you're in a mundane moment or meeting someone who's stuck in one, you can shift the energy instantly. As high-performance coach Brendon Burchard puts it, "Bring. The. Joy."

Last week at Starbucks, I noticed a slow, sad employee behind the counter. I made a playful comment, but she didn't budge. Then I went full wacky Tony on the second attempt and got her chuckling.

Always make a second attempt.

Instantly, she transformed.
Asked about my day.
Lit up.
Became a completely different person.

Over a decade of reprogramming my negative mindset about people, I've conditioned myself to be funny and silly *for* them, not against them.

Generate your joy.
Carry it wherever you go.

Old map: "Don't bother strangers. Keep your head down."

New map: "It's your job to make people smile—whether you know them or not."

FROM LOCAL TO LUXURY

Over six months, I experienced both extremes.

First, I lived like the locals.

Motorcycled through remote villages in sandals.

Climbed coconut trees.

Showered outside in my clothes when there were no enclosed stalls.

I adapted to local life: bucket showers, karaoke bars, and street food. I drew the line at balut—fertilized duck egg. Some cultural experiences can stay cultural.

Eventually, I explored the millionaire lifestyle, living in a beach house with the clear tropical ocean as my front yard.

How did I afford six months in paradise as a struggling artist with no job at the time?

Tim Ferriss taught me something in his book, *The 4-Hour Workweek:*

Geographic Arbitrage.

The setup:

- Rented out my Santa Monica office to low-budget artists (nearly double what I paid)
- Airbnb'd the Venice Beach apartment Chad and I built for that purpose

Result: My L.A. properties *that I did not own,* secretly funded my island life.

I found the beach house through a Danish guy I randomly met at a hidden restaurant near the end of the island, where the coconuts flowed like wine.

A little place called *Santander.*

He mentioned he wasn't using the house much—no internet. Perfect. I wanted to unplug.

I met him there, fell in love with it, and was introduced to the landlord, Virgie—the sweetest Filipina with a sharp sense of humor.

Next thing I knew, I was taking over the rent.

A few months later, I was tied to a tree while Karen and our friend Cherry-Mae aimed bolo knives at me—for a photoshoot I thought would make a great movie poster.

It did.

Virgie helped with set design. The locals probably thought they were watching a sacrifice.

And with the help of my neighbor Patrick, who operated camera, we got the shot.

Patrick had long silver hair, steady hands, and the quiet intensity of someone who'd lived ten lifetimes. He told me he'd worked in U.S. intelligence. Whether he shared ten percent of the truth or ninety, I'll never know.

Late nights we'd sit outside talking for hours about geopolitics, human behavior, and helicopter crashes he'd survived.

He emphasized a couple of life's golden rules: keeping your word goes a long way, and breaking someone's trust can be the end-all, be-all. I nicknamed those ideas the Patrick "We're Done" principles.

He was the kind of neighbor you're grateful to have when you're living on a remote island.

Those conversations shaped more than late-night philosophy.
They sharpened my decision-making.

Even though I wasn't supposed to live in that Santa Monica office or sublease it, I took the chance because it felt right. Would I do it that way now? No. Back then, imperfect hustle beat perfect hesitation.

I didn't have a high income or any steady income, but I knew I wanted to explore new worlds. Sometimes you gotta play dumb, be smart, and take a chance to live your dreams.

And I discovered that the Philippines isn't the scary place the news or my dad painted it to be. It's filled with some of the funniest and most present people I've ever met.

Old map: "Good life comes after decades of grinding."

New map: "Adventure and fulfillment are available now if you're creative."

FROM HER ISLAND TO HIS HOME

After filming *The Irishman* in New York, I returned to the Philippines with new clarity about what mattered: I wanted KareBear in my life permanently.

The visa process for Filipinos is brutal without marriage. So I made a practical decision that shocked even me:

"If we get married, you can come to America, then we can date and see how it really goes."

Being a film guy, I had to document my proposal. I recorded it on my phone with one hand and lifted a box with a ring in it, covered by the bed sheet, with the other.

Karen was curious and probably thought, "Wow, this guy is weird." Maybe that's what drew her to me.
It sure as heck wasn't my struggling artist's bank account.

She looked at me.
Poker face.
Then, calmly:
"Yes."

It was a moment I'll never forget because I swore I'd *never* ask anyone to marry me.

We threw an engagement party with her family and friends days later in the Philippines. It was October so I dressed as a dead magician.

After eight months of immigration legalities, Karen finally came to America in 2018 and we got married.

A few months later, *The Irishman* premiered at the Egyptian Theatre in Hollywood. She sat right beside me—the very seat I couldn't give to Chad, the guy who practically incanted me into the movie in the first place.

But hey... wife outranks hype man.

Getting married was one of the best decisions I ever made. It forced me to grow up a little—finally trading in some of that lone-wolf artist energy for something deeper, steadier, and real.

Old map: "I'm not marriage material, and I refuse government involvement."

New map: "Sometimes love makes you do things that surprise even yourself."

"The question you should be asking isn't,
'What do I want?' or 'What are my goals?'
but 'What would excite me?'"

—Tim Ferriss, *The 4-Hour Workweek*

COMING SOON

TO A LIFE CALLED YOURS

I caught a lot of lessons while traveling Asia. It untethered my soul. I stopped worrying so much. I got comfortable in the unknown. And more of that marble chipped away, revealing the real me.

That's why I shared all this—to get you to take inventory of your own trailer moments: the ones you've already lived, the ones you've delayed, and the ones you haven't yet dared to start.

Because that's the fuel. Those bold, cinematic, creative, and spontaneous moments are the heartbeat of a life worth watching.

Every expansion of your map requires the same courage: step into the unknown, stay curious instead of fearful, and collect evidence that you're more capable than you thought.

If you're still stuck, try this ridiculous but effective pattern-breaking strategy Tony Robbins teaches: stick your finger up your nose and announce your fear out loud. Seriously. You'll sound like an idiot—and that's the point.

Once you do it, you'll *hear* the absurdity, stop overthinking, and finally take the action that thrills you.

If you can't do this simple, stupid, but effective exercise, how are you going to do the brave things?

Some fears are real.
Trauma is real.
I'm not suggesting you ignore that.

If something has been weighing you down for a year or more—if it's mentally breaking you—get professional help. Therapy matters. I spent two years in it myself, doing real healing work.

But therapy is a tool, not a place to live.

At some point, we also have to question whether the fears that once protected us are still serving us now.

Some fears kept you safe.
Others kept you small.

And if a fear is no longer present in your day-to-day life, you have to ask an honest question: is this still protecting me—or is it holding me back?

Most fears are horrible hyperboles that hex your inborn heroism—tiny shadows you inflate until they black out your kid-like spirit.

Too many people lose that *magic*, and I don't want you to be one of them. You don't have to let that happen anymore. Just use the advanced finger method—stick your finger in and start chiseling away at your old patterns.

My experience in the Philippines revealed more of who I already was when I stopped living inside my old limitations.

You Become The Thing By Doing The Thing

If it's a fact—and it is—that breaking through your limitations makes you stronger and more fulfilled, then why wouldn't you want to expand your map?

Remember when you were a kid?
You'd pretend you were a doctor, a police officer, an explorer—or, if you were like me, a magician.

That childlike imagination is your creative fuel.

And now it's time to bring that imagination back.
Not to escape reality, but to expand it.

Play. Get curious. Seek new paths. Explore the unknown. Like Ed Mylett says, expand your being.

You have an unlimited map to explore. Don't let yourself—or anyone else—keep you from living free.

As you expand your map, you test your limits and push past them. All of this is prepping you for when your world flips upside down—and that's exactly what's coming next.

DIRECTOR'S COMMENTARY

You just got a feel for the fun and games stage of your life—the part where you experiment, test, fail, laugh, cry, and discover who you can become.

This is where life gets playful, and transformation sneaks in through the back door.

Remember, your map is either expanding or shrinking.
There's no neutral.

I shared my Philippines story not because I'm special, but to show that choosing your direction over someone else's fear is everything.

I traveled even when many of my friends said they would join me but didn't. I refused to let other people's incomplete maps become my reality.

Don't be a wet blanket like I was in my early twenties—cynical, closed off, suspicious of joy. That outdated version of me would've never gotten on that plane. He would've listened to Dad's "ten-years" advice and stayed comfortable.

Comfort has its place.

We all deserve it.

But it's not where you grow.

And growth is where fulfillment lives.

What's your next expansion experiment?

What adventure are you postponing?

What fear needs a finger in your nose?

Don't wait ten years.

You won't be the same person who wants to go.

You'll be the person who wishes you had.

KEY TAKEAWAYS

- Your current map is not the entire story. Update it with lived experience, not inherited fears.

- New environments literally rewire your brain for creativity and possibility.

- Imperfect hustle beats perfect hesitation every single time.

- *"Discipline weighs ounces, regret weighs tons."* —Jim Rohn

- *What if* is the slowest kind of regret. Don't wait for permission that's never coming.

- Joy lives in the spaces between plans. Edit in your trailer moments daily.

ACTION!

Welcome to fun and games.

Where you let go for a while.
Where your life map expands beyond what you currently believe is possible.

Put on your Director's hat.
Cancel your meetings.
You're gonna need a bigger card.

When you live free and make room for fun, people around you will feel your renewed aliveness and you'll become a pleasure to be around.

Pin up your card.
Expand your map.
Go. Play.

BEAT 8—MY EXPANSION

Map Limitation
Where am I generalizing, distorting, or deleting possibilities?
What adventure am I putting off—and why?

____

____

Expansion Experiment
What's one assumption about myself I could test instead of obey?
How can I make this fun instead of terrifying?

____

____

Next Trailer Moment
If my life were a movie trailer, what scene am I living next?

____

____

ACT II B
SHOOT YOUR MOViE

"80% of success is showing up."

—Woody Allen

BEAT 9

THE REVERSAL

"The pessimist sees difficulty in every opportunity.
The optimist sees opportunity in every difficulty."

—Winston Churchill

I'm standing in the international arrivals section at LAX, wearing a black cowboy hat and holding a huge handmade sign that reads "KAREN ALESER," with little hearts drawn around it.

My friend Shane is filming the whole thing.

The cowboy hat isn't a fashion statement.
It's covering my freshly shaved head from a bizarre film gig I took a couple of months earlier—just to scrape together rent money.

Then I see her.

Rolling her suitcase. Eyes scanning the crowd.

I never thought I would use the word *yearn* in a sentence, but I yearned for her. With all the visa processing and delays, I hadn't seen her in nearly eight months.

Her adorably sleepy face lit up when she spotted the ridiculous sign. She melted into my arms like the first scene of a new love story.

It felt like the opening shot of our upgraded life together.

But opening shots are designed to make you believe you know where the story is going.

THE UPGRADE

Before she arrived, I upgraded everything. No more secret office living. No more showers at the YMCA. I found a place in the Hollywood Hills.

I was pulling strings and saying yes to ridiculous gigs to get the deposit and first month's rent.

That shaved-head job? Some guy paid me good money to film him buzzing my head down to the scalp. Twenty minutes of work. Done. Then he emailed me later—apparently I went viral. I might be a fetish star somewhere, or *canceled* when someone eventually finds it.

Sometimes you take weird gigs to build something meaningful. That's what the season required.

Within a couple months of Karen arriving, and nearly 200 submissions and reach-outs later, I landed what felt like a dream job:
Director & Editor for Toon Goggles and FanLaLa TV.

Three days a week.
My own office.
An assistant editor.
Total creative freedom.
Cartoon content.
Directing a kid show with young celebrities.

For a cartoon-loving filmmaker, it was a playground with a paycheck.

I cut a *Goosebumps* promo I loved, got invited to Nickelodeon events, walked red carpets with Karen, and kept freelance work flowing on the side—editing Oxygen Network episodes and producing commercials.

We'd host movie nights in the office after hours like we owned the place. It felt stable. It felt earned. It felt like I finally cracked the code.

I remember walking into that office one morning thinking:

This is it. I figured it out.

And that's the thing about midpoints:

The moment the hero thinks they've won is usually right before everything flips.

HAPPY BIRTHDAY

One of the producers called me into his office. His expression told me everything.

"The company is shutting down. Tomorrow's your last day. There was some shady stuff happening."

The day before my birthday.
Just like that, my first taste of stability dissolved.

You're flying high in April and shot down in May. February, in my case.

Now, I'm unemployed with a wife who moved across the world believing I could provide security.

Welcome to the film industry.

YOUR TEST

In cinema, the midpoint is where everything flips. The hero who was running away starts running toward the problem. The lie they believed gets exposed. The victory they thought they won reveals itself as temporary.

Think *Star Wars*—Luke's ready to face his nemesis, then gets his hand cut off and learns Darth Vader is his father.
The Matrix—Neo thinks he's the One, then Morpheus gets captured and Neo has to decide if he actually believes it.

Rocky—he's just trying to go the distance, then realizes mid-fight he might actually win.

The reversal isn't a setback.
It's a test.
It asks: "Is this new identity real, or are you pretending?"

Your life has these moments too.
You step into your new world, gather your crew, taste success, and start believing you've figured it out.

Then the reversal hits and suddenly everything you thought was solid starts shaking.

The job you finally landed disappears.
The relationship you thought was stable fractures.
The health you took for granted fails.
The plan you committed to gets rewritten without your permission.

That's the midpoint.
And it's not here to destroy you, it's here to reveal what you're actually made of.

THE PATTERN OF REVERSALS

Sudden job loss isn't about the money. It's about the story you've been telling yourself about who you are.

For months, I'd been "Tony, the director at Toon Goggles." Now I was just "Tony, the guy who used to have a job."

Karen had settled in. She'd found her rhythm in LA, started making friends, and began building her own life around the stability I thought I could provide.

Now I had to go home and tell her that the foundation we'd been building on was actually quicksand.

I told her I'd figure it out.
But I wasn't sure I believed my own words.

We decided to visit the Philippines—her family, the islands, time to process what was next.

But underneath the tropical scenery, I was wrestling with bigger questions:

Was I actually husband material?
Could I provide the stability she deserved?
What if *"I'll figure it out"* wasn't enough this time?

When we returned to LA in early 2020, the universe decided one reversal wasn't enough.

COVID hit—the global shutdown that froze industries, closed borders, and sent the world into panic—like a second punch to an already bruised ego.

The industry I'd lost my place in shut down entirely.

But here's where the *"I'll figure it out"* mindset proved its worth.

THE GHOST HUNT

We needed money and I managed to land one gig:

B-unit DP (Cameraman) for the TV show, *Geraldo's Family Murders.*

The job?

Drive around LA at night filming the actual locations where unsolved murders happened. Karen helped out as my driver. We'd pull up to quiet suburban homes where people's lives had ended violently. I'd hop out with my camera, grab the shot guerrilla-style, then jump back in.

It was eerie work.

Quiet homes.
Dark alleys.
Neighborhoods holding tragedies no one saw coming.

Karen kept the engine running.
I kept the camera rolling.

And it reminded me of something:

Life is precious.

And if you're still fortunate to be here, walk through the darkness and remember that the story isn't over.

I wasn't finished.
I was still directing, just through a tough scene.

YOUR REVERSAL WON'T LOOK LIKE MINE

Maybe yours is:

- a breakup
- a health scare
- a business failure
- a market crash
- a friendship ending
- a dream collapsing

The pattern is always the same:

False Victory or False Defeat → Sudden Test → Identity Question

Every reversal asks:

Who are you without the external proof?

That is your MIDPOINT.

REVERSAL RECOVERY

When a reversal hits, your nervous system will try to convince you the movie is over.

It's not.

This is the beat where the *real* you steps forward.

Here's how to navigate it:

1. Immediate Response (First 24 Hours)

- Feel the shock without making permanent decisions.
- Tell at least one person in your support system what happened.
- Remind yourself: "This is a plot twist, not an ending."

This phase is about grounding.

Your only job is to stop the spiral long enough to see straight.

2. Short-Term Stabilization (First Week)

- Separate *actual* consequences from the catastrophe your mind invented.
- Identify what cannot be taken from you: your skills, your character, your connections, your resourcefulness.
- Take *one* small action that moves you forward (even if it's weird, unglamorous, or feels beneath you).

Momentum beats pride.

Reversals reward the people who move, not the ones who brood.

3. Medium-Term Adaptation (First Month)

- Look for opportunities that exist *only* because the reversal happened.
- Strengthen your "I'll figure it out" muscle by solving smaller challenges fast.
- Document what you're learning—pressure reveals patterns, and patterns reveal direction.

Adaptation isn't about bouncing back.
It's about coming back *different.*

Remember: when your world flips upside down, the wisdom only appears if you stay awake long enough to see it.

Only then can you walk the bridge to your next level.

And often, that bridge is longer and windier than you ever imagined.
Long enough to make you wonder why anyone would build it this way in the first place.

I was learning to navigate all of this through my own reversal.

A couple of months into the pandemic lockdown, it was clear that nearly every business was shut down until further notice.

But one thing that didn't stop was rent.

So I drove out to Malibu to visit a friend of mine, Stephen, for his 60th birthday, hoping to catch up and clear my head.

He owned a stunning property overlooking the Pacific Ocean, but a year earlier local wildfires had burned down a huge chunk of it, including his pool house. What used to be a peaceful backyard oasis now looked like the opening shot of a post-apocalyptic film: charred beams, cracked concrete, and a drained lap pool filled with ash and debris.

If I hadn't been desperately scrambling for work, housing, and money, I would've asked him if I could film a movie down there.

Instead, we stood there staring at the wreckage in silence. Him frustrated, me quietly calculating my next move in life.

Then something sparked.

"Stephen," I said, "what if I rebuild this into a tiny home?"

He turned to me, squinting those piercing blue eyes like he was deciding whether I was brilliant or insane.

"I'll pay for materials. Do the labor. My wife and I can live here for a couple of years—rent-free, or until you get sick of me—and you'll end up with your property rebuilt."

A beat.

Then he nodded.

We were moving to Malibu. Just like that.

I didn't know it then, but this was the moment in the movie where the hero thinks they've found a lifeline, but the audience can already sense something's coming.

Malibu was going to test everything I believed about myself.

DIRECTOR'S COMMENTARY

Do you want to go out like this?

No.

The midpoint is where your life-movie earns its ending. Without your reversal, there's no proof of transformation—just a lucky break that could disappear at any moment.

When everything you built gets shaken, you discover what's actually solid.

The skills nobody can take away.
The relationships that stay when you lose status.
The identity that exists independent of external validation.

This beat taught me that success isn't about reaching a destination—it's about how you handle the moment when that destination gets yanked away.

Do you collapse?
Or do you adapt, pivot, and keep directing?

The universe doesn't care that you finally found stability.
It cares whether you can stay in the Director's chair when the script gets rewritten without your permission.

My "I'll figure it out" mindset got its biggest test yet. Losing that job was about to force me into the most creative period of my life.

Sometimes the best scenes come after everything falls apart.

The reversal isn't punishment—it's the rewrite that reveals your true character.

KEY TAKEAWAYS

- Reversals test identity: Who are you when the external proof disappears?
- Adaptation beats resistance: Your job isn't to prevent reversals, but to navigate them.
- Dark work has purpose—the uncomfortable scenes teach crucial lessons.
- "I'll figure it out" is a superpower. Resourcefulness outranks any perfect plan.

ACTION!

The fun and games are over.

Don't lose focus.
Double down.

This is where you realize time is precious.
And so is the messy middle of your story.

Locate evidence of adaptation—proof of the inner quality you can trust when things go wrong.

Fill out the next card and pin it beside the others on your Director's Board.

Reversals don't end your movie.
They reveal your backbone.
When one hits, you adapt.

Get to work.

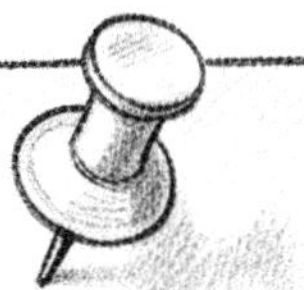

BEAT 9—MY REVERSAL

The Turning Point
What recent false victory made me feel secure, but was actually fragile? Or what false defeat felt crushing, but wasn't the end of my story?

____

____

The Truth Beneath the Moment
What uncomfortable truth was exposed and what behavior proves I stay resourceful under pressure?

____

____

The Reversal Reveal
What skill, relationship, or inner quality showed up when things flipped?

____

____

BEAT 10

THE PRESSURE COOKER

"Welcome to the party, pal!"

—John McClane, *Die Hard*

I've never told this to *anyone*. It's embarrassing—but you need to know I wasn't living some Malibu dream. Not even close.

Karen and I moved into Stephen's office in the house during the build. Everything we owned was crammed into that one room. The overflow spilled into the bathroom. Random supplies, laundry, and all our kitchen gear were stacked wherever they could fit.

One afternoon, a friend and his wife came by to help me carry a heavy sliding glass door down that winding 200-foot trail to the tiny house structure. As a thank-you, Karen made her homemade Filipino soup. That's her love language.

We had nowhere to cook except in the bathroom, so we heated the soup on a hot plate balanced on the counter.

While it was warming, nature called. I figured I had a minute alone.

Wrong.

My friend's wife walked right in—probably thinking it led to a kitchen—and opened the door to *me*. Sitting on the toilet. Mid-business.

We locked eyes.

It was the kind of silent horror moment where your whole body turns white. I don't remember if she glanced left and saw the soup simmering feet away from the toilet, but I do know I was humiliated.

I'm sure other people have had it worse, but in that moment I didn't feel like a man. I felt like a failure with no class.

It was a signal.
Loud and clear.

It yelled, "You're capable of more. Reassess everything, raise your standards, *and lock bathroom doors!*"

For the record, we have a real kitchen now.

We never saw those friends again.

BAD GUYS CLOSE IN

In filmmaking, this is where the stakes rise and the tension builds. The hero's external enemies attack while their internal weaknesses are exposed.

It's not one problem—it's *every* problem at once.

In one of my favorite films by Scorsese, *Goodfellas*, Henry Hill's paranoia hits a breaking point.

The FBI is closing in.
His drug operation is unraveling.
Everyone in his crew becomes a potential rat.

The same cocaine-fueled recklessness that once made him successful now makes him sloppy. He's cooking dinner, making deals, and looking over his shoulder every second—moving fast, thinking he's in control, while everything quietly collapses around him.

The pressure comes from everywhere.

Your life has these moments too.
Multiple external crises expose your internal weaknesses, while your character flaws make everything worse.

For me, that pressure cooker was Malibu, 2020.

Everything was closing in.

It felt like trying to solve a Rubik's Cube while riding a unicycle through a hallway of people shoving you from both sides.

Work had vanished.
We were living on credit.

I was building a tiny home with my bare hands.
Lugging lumber and hammering boards.
Racing to finish the house so we could escape Stephen's small office, where the bathroom doubled as our kitchen.

I had sworn I'd never live in an office again.
Let alone with my new wife.
Yet there I was.

Then there was Armen.
My best friend since we were fifteen.

We'd had a major falling out years earlier. Now we were cautiously reconnecting through a challenge that demanded balance, patience, and play.

That reconnection wasn't simple. It was emotional and it was stressful.

This was someone I'd spent over a decade with. I'd lived in his house for six months. His family felt like my second family. So when things fell apart between us, it wasn't a disagreement—it was a rupture.

The kind that leaves things unsaid.
The kind where forgiveness isn't instant, and trust has to be rebuilt slowly.

But we had history.
Back then, we made ridiculous films together.
We got in trouble together.

We pushed each other creatively and tested boundaries like only teenage boys do.

And remember Beat 5, where I mentioned writing, producing, and shooting my cousin's proof-of-concept film?

That wasn't a past crisis. It was unfolding at the exact same time.
It was familial pressure with real stakes and no easy answers.

My cousin deserves credit. She always believed in me. She trusted me with the film, rooted for my career, and gave me an opportunity. But she was also overwhelmed on her first directing project, burning through money faster than I could pour concrete. She wanted total creative support. I wanted stability for my wife.

The project jeopardized our relationship.

Neither of us handled everything perfectly, but it taught me something essential:

Love isn't saying yes to everything. Sometimes love is setting a boundary.

All these pressures—financial, creative, emotional, marital, relational— were about to collide into the most intense identity test of my life.

PROBLEMS IN PARADISE

Living in my Malibu creation was like glamping in a beautiful death trap. Every day we had to keep an eye out for danger.

The Rattlesnake Situation

Multiple venomous neighbors slithered through my construction materials.

Karen was already terrified of snakes, and I had basically built our little Malibu dream house in rattlesnake territory.

Adult rattlers.

Baby rattlers.

She'd scream just stepping outside.

I kept having the morbid thought:
What if this crazy project gets her killed by a rattlesnake?

The Wind Incident

One morning, I left for an acting job at 4 a.m. Not long after, Karen woke to winds so violent she thought the house might blow over. One of Stephen's dogs, Bella, came barking to "rescue" her, and she hiked up to the main house in her pajamas.

Maybe the city inspector had been right.
Maybe I should have hired an architect.

The Water Bottle Ant Situation

Nothing quite like waking up thirsty in the middle of the night, taking a big gulp from your water bottle, and getting a mouthful of ants.

The Electricity Issue

We had to put our mini fridge outside Stephen's bunker-like man cave, tucked into the hillside between his house and the tiny home—the only place with electricity. Midnight snack? Night hike through rattlesnake land.

Looking back, I can't believe I put my wife through that. But she stayed. That's love… or maybe she's as crazy as me.

The Not So Friendly Notice

The house build was pure right-brain madness.

I drew it, envisioned it, measured and planned it like a film project. I got the right tools, obsessed over YouTube tutorials, and executed with the passion of someone making their Directorial debut.

I built about 85% of it myself over six months.

Eventually, I had to call in an expert. My friend Cyrus—who can build and fix anything—helped during the final stages over several weekends. Working alongside him bonded us in a way years of casual friendship never had. He showed up with skill. I showed up with top-quality pizza.

Karen helped with painting, turning our tiny house into something that actually felt like a home.

My big mistake?

I used my creative brain and completely ignored my logical one.

Left-brain Tony would've asked, "Hey, do I need permits for this?" Right-brain Tony said, "Permits are for people who think small!"

My dad had joked earlier, "I've been trying to figure out how to get a house in Malibu since the 1970s, and you did it in six months!" My lack of planning got me in, but it also got me in trouble.

There's a sweet spot between analysis paralysis and reckless action.

I missed it completely.

And that's when the real trouble arrived.

October 2020.

Six months into construction.
We'd just finished painting the exterior.
The house was essentially done. It was beautiful, functional enough, and everything I'd envisioned.
We were finally exhaling.

Then the pink letter with the city seal showed up taped to Stephen's front door.

This structure was built without proper permits.
You have 30 days to make it compliant or face legal action.

Pit. In. Stomach.

Stephen and I scrambled.
We called architects, city planners, permit specialists. We thought we could get a retroactive permit like some of his neighbors had.

But this was California...
$25,000 minimum to make it legal. Plus, we would need to rebuild the structure to code.

It would take money we absolutely didn't have.

FINDING BALANCE WHILE LOSING IT

During the most stressful construction periods, my friend Armen and I found some balance in our rekindled relationship—literally.

I taught him to unicycle in beach parking lots.
Two grown men learning equilibrium while my actual life was falling apart.

"This is impossible!" he'd yell, falling for the bajillionth time.

"Possible it is," I'd reply, circling him like a Jedi master.

We got so good we could ride down stairs.

Pure joy in the chaos.

No film drama.

No creative disagreements.

Just two friends doing something completely ridiculous and loving every minute of it.

It was ironic: I was teaching someone to find their balance while losing mine. But the physical and mental rhythm of the challenge kept me going.

But as the permit situation became impossible, Karen and I started having those "natural arguments" that happen when Malibu dream houses collide with legal reality.

She was probably questioning why she'd married an unstable guy like me. I was starting to conclude that I wasn't able to take care of the girl who moved across the world for me.

"What now?" she asked.

I stared at the house I'd built with my hands. "I don't know… yet."

(Adding the word "yet" after something you don't know gives your brain a crack of hope that you'll figure it out eventually. Word choice is a superpower.)

That's when she decided to fly to a friend in another state—a woman she'd met once during the immigration process but stayed in touch with over the phone.

Turns out, the friend was a complete nutjob—bipolar and unstable. Karen's "escape" spiraled fast, and she needed a safer option.

So she flew to my mom's house in South Carolina instead.

For the first time, she was meeting my family—alone, without me to buffer anything. She was scared, shy, overwhelmed… but she did it.

Meanwhile, I was in Malibu trying to solve the unsolvable. I was frustrated that my choices had separated us, but proud of her courage at the same time.

We were apart because of the mess I got us into.

This wasn't a Malibu dream anymore—*it was a Malibu nightmare.* And I needed to wake up.

I had to make a clear decision. One that would release the pressure, put me back in the Director's chair, and keep me moving on my ambitious journey to make the most of my life and still have strong relationships.

WHAT'S YOUR PRESSURE COOKER?

I know yours isn't building a house in the middle of snake paradise without permits.

But you have your own pressure cooker, your own moment where everything closes in at once. That's what happens when you move through life with goals bigger than the people around you.

The stakes rise.
The challenges compound.
And suddenly, the gap between who you are and who you're becoming demands to be closed.
Right now.

When that moment hits, your internal world gets loud.
Your creativity can morph into recklessness.
Your independence can turn into isolation.
Your confidence can wobble into self-doubt.

And your passion—if you're not careful—can tilt into a negative obsession.

The pressure cooker tests your identity.

But this is the point.

Your life becomes the best movie you'll ever experience when you stay in the Director's chair—especially when everything around you is falling apart.

To live intentionally, confidently, and joyfully—even in chaos—that's the real skill you're building.
Equanimity.

You don't need a perfect life.
You need clarity and courage when all hell breaks loose.

Your pressure cooker moments can break you down or build you up.

Make your decision.
Cut everything else off.

PRESSURE MANAGEMENT

When everything closes in, the first shock is always external.

The permit inspectors. The financial strain. The family drama. The unexpected chaos.

But the real antagonist usually isn't out there. It's the part of you that reacts instead of responds: impatience, pride, poor planning, or the belief that asking for help means weakness. Pressure has a way of revealing exactly what you've avoided dealing with.

When your world gets noisy, the only way forward is clarity.
Not perfection. Clarity.

Pressure forces you to see what actually matters, what can wait, and what was never yours to carry in the first place. Some problems demand immediate action. Others are discomfort disguised as urgency. And some crises aren't even yours—they're other people trying to hand you their chaos.

In the middle of all of this, you need something that brings you back to center.

For me, it was unicycling with Armen in empty beach parking lots while my life was falling apart. It made no sense on paper, which is probably why it worked. Pure joy. Zero stakes. A reminder that I was still allowed to feel alive while everything else felt like it was collapsing.

That's the strange gift of pressure.
It exposes your emotional defaults.
And it gives you a chance to rewrite them.

When the permit notice landed and the floor dropped out from under me, I could have spiraled. Instead, I let the pit in my stomach sit there long enough for curiosity to enter. What's this here to teach me? What is this preparing me for?

The Stoics call it *amor fati*.
Love your fate.

Not because it's easy.
Because it's the only way to stay in the Director's chair when the script suddenly changes.

DIRECTOR'S COMMENTARY

You will face moments in life that feel like Malibu—messy, humbling, expensive, exposing, and loud. There's no universe where you walk through that kind of pressure unchanged.

Looking back, I'll admit there were *many* days I felt like a loser. Days when I questioned every choice that led me there. Days when I wanted to quit, crawl under a metaphorical rock, and pretend none of it was happening.

But I didn't. And I'm damn proud of that.

I stayed in the discomfort.
I stayed in my own growth.

That alone built more real confidence than any job, praise, or lucky break ever has. It's the kind of confidence you only earn when life has you backed into a corner and you still choose to step forward.

Yeah, I made some moronic mistakes along the way. I ignored permits. I lived in an office again. I lost fifteen grand building something the city eventually made me demolish.

But the pressure cooker doesn't destroy you—it reveals you.

Your strengths get exposed.
Your weaknesses get exposed.
Your blind spots, old identities, and emotional defaults all surface in the heat.

Creativity becomes recklessness when pushed too far.
Independence turns into isolation.
Resilience morphs into stubbornness.
Confidence slips into arrogance.

These aren't flaws. They're features... until they're not.

Malibu handed me all of that at once. It cracked me open in every direction. And as much as I hated it, I needed it.

Pressure-cooker moments force you to confront the inner villain who's been quietly directing your life from the shadows.

If I were with you inside your pressure-cooker moment right now, I'd punch you playfully in the arm, crack a dumb joke, make an obnoxious sound effect—anything to get you to laugh. Because the moment your state shifts, your intelligence comes back online, and suddenly the impossible becomes solvable.

But I'm not there.
So you have to do that for yourself.

I'm grateful Malibu happened.
If it hadn't, I wouldn't have the stories, the tools, the humility, or the depth I have now. I wouldn't have the relationships that strengthened because of that chaos.

I definitely wouldn't have the new level of confidence that can only come from being caught on a toilet by your friend's wife while your soup simmers on a hot plate in the bathroom.

Okay—embarrassing image aside, I genuinely felt like the main character in a film being dragged through hell because the transformation on the other side mattered that much.

Pressure.
Breakdowns that become breakthroughs.
A character arc you can look back on and say, "Yeah… I earned that.".
Don't abandon the Director's chair.

KEY TAKEAWAYS

- Equanimity is a skill. Staying steady when everything shakes is something you train, not something you're born with.
- Boundaries protect relationships.
- Playfulness keeps you sane. Joy isn't a luxury in chaos; it's a stabilizer. `

ACTION!

It's time to use the pressure to your advantage.
This one can save you months.

Take a few deep breaths... and begin.

Please *schedule your stabilizer in your calendar* so you don't explode. We all need activities that help us get into a flow state, reset, and experience bliss.

Pressure requires your presence, not panic. Let it teach you what comfort never could.

Pin this card beside the others on your Director's Board.

The bad guys in life don't end you—they test your endurance.
Pressure doesn't just crush—it crystallizes.
It molds the version of you who can hold more and create more.

You handled the reversal. You're adapting under pressure. Now comes the collapse: the moment when everything you built starts bursting at the seams.

Don't give up.
This is where the real transformation begins.

BEAT 10—MY PRESSURE TEST

Identifying Pressure
What are the top three pressures in my life right now?
Circle the one that would cause the most damage if
ignored.

    1.________________________

    2.________________________

    3.________________________

What Am I Missing?
Am I lacking creativity or strategy? Which internal flaw
is fueling this?
impatience · pride · isolation · refusing help

____

____

Stabilizer
What is my "unicycle"—a joyful, pressure-free activity
that resets my nervous system?

____

BEAT 11
THE COLLAPSE

"Let misfortune fall upon me rather than
upon another, for I know I can bear it."

—Marcus Aurelius

I hand my friend the cash to destroy the
house I built with my bare hands.

The same house where Karen and I briefly shared our first real home. The same house that's about to become a pile of debris.

"You sure about this?" Armen asks.

I look up, still in mourning.

"Yeah. The city's forcing us to tear it down. Stephen owns the land, California doesn't care unless you—"

"—I've been waiting years for this moment!" Armen cuts me off, grinning with pure, unfiltered joy as he fires up his excavator like a kid on Christmas morning.

CRUNCH.
CLANK.
SNAP.

It's painful.
So I leave for a while.

When I come back, the walls are collapsed, stacked on themselves. Devastation mixed with…

Relief.

The fight was over.
No more notices.
No more pretending this tiny house is the answer.

Sometimes destruction is freedom.

Several months.
Thousands of dollars.
A dream of proving that a struggling artist could carve out a Malibu view.

Demolished in a couple of hours.

This was supposed to be proof.
Something permanent.
Something that lasted.

Now it's a mound of splintered wood and twisted metal.
And I still have to pay the junk haulers.

ALL IS LOST

In cinema, "All Is Lost" is the moment when the shit hits the fan and the hero loses it all.

Not one thing—*everything*.

In *Rocky*, Rocky Balboa takes a brutal beating from Apollo Creed. His face is destroyed, his body is broken, and he realizes he can't win. But he keeps getting back up. Not because he thinks he can win, but because staying down isn't who he is.

The fight isn't about winning anymore.
It's about proving he can take the hit and still stand.

External collapse reveals what's indestructible inside you.

For me, that moment was watching my house become rubble while standing next to a friend who was enjoying every second of the demolition.

Beat 11 isn't about more bad guys.
It's the moment their pressure breaks the system.
Everything stops working at once.

Think over your life as I describe the moments in mine that collided simultaneously:

The Housing Crisis: Legal compliance meant a new build plus new plans we couldn't afford. Goodbye, tiny house.

The Financial Collapse: Savings gone to materials, demolition costs, and nowhere to live.

The Relationship Strain: My wife crossed the world for stability. I delivered chaos.

The Identity Crisis: Without title, house, or plan—who was I?

A guy watching his Malibu dream house get torn down by his friend.

After the house was destroyed, we retreated to Stephen's extra room yet again. That evening, Karen found me staring at the pile of rubble through the window.

"What are you thinking about?" she asked.

"How I convinced you to move across the world for this."

"For what?"

"Nothing. No job. No house. No clear direction. You could have stayed in the Philippines and had a better life."

A few beats passed. The air thick with everything unsaid.

"You have resilience."

That conversation didn't fix everything immediately. But it planted a seed that would eventually grow into my future.

When you hit rock bottom, you're forced to get creative.

The demolition was part of the collapse. What came next was the aftermath.

During the chaos, we were able to escape for a short while and visit my mom in South Carolina. She was one of the few people who wasn't letting COVID sensationalism scare her out of loving her family.

But when we crossed back into California, reality was waiting.

The day we flew back to LA, Stephen texted us. His daughter was visiting and staying in her old bedroom—the bathroom connected directly to the office we'd been sleeping in.

He didn't want her to feel uncomfortable sharing a space with people she didn't know. So we couldn't move back in until she left. And no one knew when that would be.

I started making calls to local family members.

"We need a place to crash for a few weeks while we figure things out…"

Call by call, COVID fears closed doors.

I would have called my cousin, but the tension around our film project was still hanging in the air, and I figured she needed space from my chaotic life.

I didn't get resentful, I got resourceful.

When you think you're out of options, you're not.

As Alex Banayan explains in his book *The Third Door,*

"If you're willing to jump out of line, run down the alley, bang on the door a hundred times, crack open the window, sneak through the kitchen—there's always, *always* the third door."

We had three options:

1. Beg family

    I don't beg

2. Rent an overpriced Airbnb in Los Angeles

    We couldn't afford it

That left one more door.

¡VIVA MÉXICO!

I called the most adventurous guy I know—Armen.

"Want to split living costs in Mexico for a few weeks until Stephen's daughter leaves? Our money will go way further there than any LA Airbnb."

"Yeah, dude," he said without hesitation.

Within days, we were carpooling south across the border in Armen's white Honda. Two Americans and my Filipina wife, armed with questionable Spanish skills and a plan that made perfect sense to us.

A week into our Mexican adventure, Armen was driving us down a bustling street. I was in the passenger seat, Karen was in the back, eyeing a fruit stand stacked with mangos, pineapples, limes, and chile.

"Oooo, look!" Karen said.

"Pull over, we'll be quick," I told Armen.

Karen and I got out while Armen stayed in the car.

I stumbled through broken Spanish to the vendor finally using my high school skills. Karen and I crossed back with our chile-lime fruit. I opened the back door for her, and she slipped inside. I opened the passenger door, leaned halfway in, and...

There were two random guys sitting in the front!

Where the hell was Armen?

"Hola," he said, smiling.

"Uh... mi amigo era aquí?" I said in butchered Spanish.

We all laughed. And right then, Armen pulled up beside us—in an almost identical white Honda—having watched the entire thing unfold.

When life feels automatic, that's when you drift.
Pay attention especially in the moments that seem easy.

Later that night: Mexican wrestling masks, ocean view, Armen and me wrestling on the hotel floor while Karen laughed at us.

We were living like royalty on a budget: high-quality hotels, empty restaurants, waiters treating us like VIPs because we were the only tourists brave enough to be there during the COVID pandemic.

"You two are ridiculous," Karen said through her laughter.

"This is what happens when your life falls apart and you decide to make it an adventure instead of a tragedy," I said through the mask.

Well... okay, I didn't actually say that.

But it *would've* been a perfect line.

For the first week, we lived it up. Then we extended our stay for three more weeks. Ziplines. Ocean views. Our money went further there than it ever could in LA. It saved our budget and our morale.

Instead of drowning in expensive American chaos, we chose something that made us feel alive.

But all adventures end—and when reality knocks, it knocks hard.

After Stephen's daughter went back to college, we moved into the guest room again. That's when the real processing began.

Processing is another word for reflecting.

When I hear the word reflecting, I think about Marcus Aurelius.

He lived nearly 2,000 years ago as the Stoic emperor of Rome, long before cinema existed. But I wonder if he ever saw his life like a movie? Did he ever imagine himself as the protagonist in his own story, making choices that would echo through history?

He couldn't have known his *Meditations* would be read by millions. He was just writing to himself, trying to make sense of loss, power, and mortality.

Research in positive psychology shows that people who see themselves as the hero—not the victim—recover faster and grow stronger under pressure.

It makes sense.

Marcus figured this out. He chose to bear misfortune, reflect, and act—not because he had to, but because he knew growth lived on the other side.

That's the shift.
That's the collapse teaching you who you actually are.

"It ain't about how hard you hit.
It's about how hard you can get hit
and keep moving forward."

—Rocky Balboa, *Rocky*

THE DARK GIFT

Sometimes you have to change lenses for different scenes.
I've learned these moments are not punishment. They're preparation.

Everything I thought defined me was taken away.
Everything I thought made me successful as a man was stripped down to nothing.

But what remained?

My enthusiasm for challenge.
The skills no one could take away.
The resilience I'd built through every previous breakdown.
The weird sense of humor that kept me sane (Mexican wrestling masks go a long way).
The ability to see stories in the wreckage.
The strong wife who didn't give up on me when times were tough.

Standing in that pile of apocalyptic-looking rubble where our house used to be, I had a thought that felt more like surrender than revelation:

If I can survive this, I'm tougher than I thought.
But I'm tired of proving it.

After my build-and-destroy-a-house-in-Malibu fiasco, life was pure survival mode: odd jobs, regrouping, piecing things together. The idea of "figuring it out" felt exhausting.

But slowly—so slowly I almost didn't notice—new ideas started bubbling up.

During the last couple months of being in Malibu, a thought started forming. Not a grand vision. A quiet whisper:

What if the skills that got me through this breakdown could help others break through?

What if the collapse was the education for my real work?

The house was gone.

Something else was trying to be born.

DIRECTOR'S COMMENTARY

The collapse can clarify you—or kill you.

It takes a reframe and mitigation—how you respond, adjust, and protect your energy—if you want to come out alive. The most effective way to handle adversity is to find a way to make it a little fun. Add some color. Gamify it where you can. Step away when needed and hit your version of "Mexico" to recharge.

This doesn't mean being irresponsible. It means getting creative.
The collapse comes one way or another.

It doesn't care about your plans. It doesn't ask permission. It just arrives. And when it does, your only job is to stay in the story long enough to see what comes next.

This beat taught me something brutal: you can go *all in* and still lose. You can build with your hands, pour your heart into it, sacrifice for months, and watch it all become rubble in hours.

It's a paradox: sometimes you have to lose everything to discover what nobody can take away.

Marcus Aurelius knew it. Rocky Balboa knew it. And now you know it too.

KEY TAKEAWAYS

- Loss reveals essence: what remains when everything else is stripped away?

- Family can't always save you: self-reliance becomes non-negotiable

- Humor heals: finding lightness in darkness is a survival skill

- Destruction can be preparation: sometimes life clears space for your real beginning

- Perspective shifts everything: change your lens, change your story

- Resilience is reframing: seeing yourself as the hero, not the victim, changes recovery speed

- The third option always exists: when stuck, think outside the box

ACTION!

When people parrot the hollow motivational phrase, *"you've got this,"* it mildly pisses me off.

There's no specificity. No focus. Just air.

No.
You've *got to do this* next defined step. The one that moves the needle right now. That's how new muscles are built.

Finish your next card and pin it to your Director's Board.

Your collapse isn't your conclusion—it's your compost.

Everything is gone. You're still here. That matters more than you think.

The darkest hour isn't the end. It's the doorway.

BEAT 11—MY COLLAPSE

Demolition Moment
What's the thing I've built that I'm most afraid of losing?

———————————————————————————

Who's Really There?
Who will help me if this collapses? What happens if they can't *or won't*?

———————————————————————————

———————————————————————————

Third Option
If my first two options fail, where's the third door?

———————————————————————————

———————————————————————————

What Still Stands
If all of this disappeared, what about me would still work?

———————————————————————————

———————————————————————————

THE MALiBU DEPRESSiON

> "Trade your expectations for appreciation."
>
> —Tony Robbins

It was miserably hot.

We were back to living on a pity favor—crammed into Stephen's small office-turned-guest room, barely big enough for our belongings, no air conditioning.

You're living in America's idea of paradise, but you can't shake the thought that you've failed the one person who moved across the world to build a life with you.

"You still awake?" I whispered to Karen.

"Yeah. Why is it so hot in here?"

"We could lay a blanket out on the beach?"

That night, we ended up sleeping on the sand, moonlit waves acting as white noise. Karen curled up in one arm and my baseball bat in the other. Just in case. It was a public beach.

As she drifted off, I lay there half-awake in that strange space between reflecting and protecting.

The same questions looped:
What am I supposed to do now?
Am I actually talented, or am I fooling myself?

What kind of husband can't provide basic stability?
Would she be happier with someone who had a normal life and a normal career?

Every social media scroll showed former classmates buying houses, getting promotions, looking like they had their shit together.

Meanwhile, I was unemployed, sweating through the night, wondering if every choice I made was wrong.

Yeah, I'd lived some meaningful adventures.
They just didn't pay the bills.
Yet.

My days collapsed into a depressing routine:

9:00 AM—Wake up staring at where my house used to be.

10:00 AM—Matcha tea with Karen. Both of us pretending we weren't worried about money.

11:00 AM—Check emails for work. Nothing.

12:00 PM—Walk around Malibu feeling like a fraud. Everyone else driving Teslas to million-dollar homes. Me wondering how long before we'd have to leave.

2:00 PM—Remember Karen mentioning she wants kids. I silently calculate how impossible that feels with our current finances.

3:00 PM—Apply for jobs I don't want and probably won't get.

5:00 PM—Make dinner with clean, healthy ingredients. The one thing I can still provide. Food mattered to us.

7:00 PM—Obsess over cryptocurrency videos hoping I'll figure out how to get crypto rich.

9:00 PM—Numb out to Netflix, pretending I'm studying filmmaking.

2:00 AM—Lie in bed wondering about the future.

I became a recluse again. I didn't ask anyone for help.

From the outside, it probably looked like we were "living it up in Malibu." From the inside, I was being dragged through the F.U.D.

THE BRIDGE

In cinema, Beat 12 is called the Dark Night of the Soul: the reflective, do-or-die moment where nothing seems capable of solving the central problem.

In *It's a Wonderful Life*, George Bailey stands on a bridge in the snow, ready to jump.

He's lost everything.
His business is failing.
He's about to be arrested.
His dreams of travel died years ago.

He believes his family would be better off with the insurance money than with him.
He's convinced the world would be better off if he'd never been born.

That's the moment when you consider removing yourself from your own story.

I never stood on a literal bridge.

I did sink back into the nihilism I thought I'd outgrown—wanting to disappear.

I had many 2 a.m. moments staring at the ceiling, wondering if Karen would be better off without me.
If my family would feel relief instead of worry.
If the world would even notice whether I stayed or left.

That's how you know you've hit the Dark Night of the Soul:

When your solution is to remove yourself from the equation.

When the real question becomes:

Do I stay in the story—or remove myself from it?

THE NUMBING TEMPTATIONS

When your soul feels crushed, everything becomes a potential escape:

- Binge-watching Netflix until your eyes burn
- Researching how to "get rich" when you don't have much to invest
- Staying in bed until the afternoon because facing the day feels impossible
- Picking fights with the people closest to you—because at least anger feels like something

I tried all of it.

What helped wasn't escaping.
It was interrupting the spiral.

Walking.
Gratitude.
Creative thinking about an exciting future.
Deciding—consciously—what things meant and what actions I could take next.

Many of history's most innovative minds walked. There are countless anecdotes—and growing research—showing that walking helps declutter the mind and unlock creative thinking.

When the loop starts, return to these anchors:

This is temporary. You'll figure it out. Focus on what you can control.

The key isn't "thinking positive."
It's thinking better. Acting better. Choosing better.

At first, that means breaking autopilot—catching the loop and consciously redirecting it.

Your thoughts will run on repeat whether you choose them or not.
Choose carefully.

THE VISION BOARD THAT DISAPPEARED

You know that scene in *Back to the Future* where Marty's hand starts disappearing from the photograph because his parents might not get together?

That's what happened to my vision.

I couldn't even find my vision board anymore—not literally, but metaphorically. All those goals I'd written down. All those dreams I'd been so certain about. They felt like they were fading from existence.

The house I'd built? Gone.
The stable income? Gone.
The man I thought I was becoming? Disappearing—*just like Marty's hand.*

But as every Director knows, when the picture goes dark, it's not the end. It's the transition.

Somewhere between the demolished house and the family rejection, something fundamental changed in how I approached life.

The old Tony would've kept charging ahead with pure right-brain energy, trusting that passion and creativity would solve everything.

The new Tony realized something sobering:

When you get married, you can't make random, kid-like decisions all the time.

Don't get me wrong, I still planned to keep playfulness as the path and curiosity as the compass. But I needed to turn on the left-brain switch.

Play the game smarter.
Not harder.

I made a philosophy shift:

Old approach:
"I can handle anything."
(pure force)

New approach:
"I can figure this out—but first, what can I learn from this?
What's best for the life I want?
The person I want to become?
Let's think this through."
(intuition + strategy + confidence)

Core belief:
Failure is feedback.
You take action to get feedback.
Feedback builds competency.
Competency builds confidence.
Then the loop repeats.

During one of those beach reflection sessions, I called my friend Brandon.

"Hey, we're moving to Cincinnati."

"Really? When?"

I still have love for my hometown.

But did I really want to live and die in L.A.?
Did I want to raise kids in a cutthroat concrete jungle?

Brandon had previously shown me Cincinnati was full of friendly people, good energy, and most importantly for my wife, incredible food that actually met L.A. standards.

When I told Karen the plan, she smiled and said,

"Another road trip?"

That's why I love her.

She wasn't staying out of obligation.
She was choosing the adventure with me.

That moment helped me realize Memento Mori isn't "remember you must die so be reckless." It's "remember you must die so live strong, show up responsibly, and build something that matters while you're here."

Because how you live creates a ripple.

Like when George Bailey stood on that bridge. Clarence didn't just save him. He showed him what the world would look like if he'd never been born. Every life he'd touched. Every moment of kindness. Every sacrifice.

All of it mattered more than he could see in his darkest hour.

You don't need an angel to show you this.
You need to remember: someone is always watching you.
Not in a creepy surveillance way, but in a "you're the role model someone needs" way.

Maybe it's your kids watching how you handle failure.
Maybe it's a coworker noticing how you stay kind when stressed.
Maybe it's a stranger who sees you smile despite everything and thinks, "If they can keep going, maybe I can too."

Someone is watching how you handle your life.
You are the role model.
Live beyond yourself.

The moment you realize someone's counting on you to keep showing up—even if you don't know who they are yet—that's when the dark night of the soul starts to lift.

"Hope is a good thing, maybe the best of things, and no good thing ever dies."

—Andy Dufresne, *The Shawshank Redemption*

THE EGO TRAP

You think you're the only one who's lost a home?
Who's broke and scared?
Who's wondering if they made every wrong choice?

No.

That's your ego talking.

The moment your ego asks, *"Why am I not where I SHOULD be?"* That's when you get lost.

Your ego loves the drama of feeling special in your suffering. It compares your struggle to everyone else's highlight reel and convinces you that you're uniquely broken.

You're not.
You're universally human.

Everyone who's ever directed their life instead of drifting through it has faced a version of this beat.

The difference between the ones who made it and the ones who didn't? The ones who made it stopped listening to the ego's victim story and started asking better questions.

Not, *"Why is this happening to me?"*
But, *"What is this preparing me for?"*

The fact that you're still here—still reading, still showing up—is evidence.

Being depressed in paradise taught me something brutal *and freeing:*
Your internal state determines your experience, not your circumstances.
You can be miserable in Malibu or peaceful in *another* small office.
It's always an inside job.

If you persist...
You give yourself a chance to succeed.

If you stay stuck...
You will live a life of desperation until the bitter end, full of regret.

That kind of living is hell on earth.

Life is short and time is precious.
You will take your last breath one day—make that day matter by living fully until you get there.

THE SUBTLE SHIFT

The dark night of the soul doesn't end with a dramatic revelation.
It ends with a subtle shift.

One morning, walking the beach after another night of reflecting and protecting, I realized I wasn't searching for answers anymore.
I was just walking.
Fast.

When I walk like that, it either looks like I have an important meeting to get to or like I'm part of a crazed cult about to board a metaphorical spaceship.

That walk became its own meditation.

Somewhere between steps, *I untethered my soul.* I knew the worst was over. Not because my circumstances had changed. They hadn't.

I was still unemployed.
Still uncertain.
Still figuring things out.

But I was no longer afraid of not knowing.

After months of those beach sessions, the questions softened.
Desperation turned into curiosity.

I have all these scenes.
All this data.
What could I do with it?

As a Director, the possibilities are limitless.
I didn't intellectualize it then, but something fundamental shifted.

I've always seen my life like a movie, but this time, I saw this period as raw footage: scenes to study, noise to trim, meaning to re-edit.

When you learn to face your F.U.D. through the Director's lens, you become available for possibilities you couldn't see before.

That's the gateway to emotional freedom and self-mastery.

DIRECTOR'S COMMENTARY

This is the moment you *want* to jump off the cliff.

You're one decision away from breaking, or building.
You're standing in the space between who you were and who you're becoming.

This period isn't meant to be fixed quickly. It's meant to be experienced consciously.

So let yourself feel it—but don't live there.

You're allowed to grieve, be angry, and be exhausted.
But don't confuse *processing* with *wallowing*.

Every morning you wake up is a gift.
Every person counting on you is a responsibility.
Every possibility ahead is a privilege.

Expression without impression leads to depression.

So express.

Someone needs you to make a come back.
Whether that's a person, a future version of yourself, or even your dog—it doesn't matter. Step down from the pity pedestal, re-enter the story, and be the role model you were meant to be.

George Bailey didn't jump off that bridge.
And you're not jumping off yours either.

You're crossing it.

KEY TAKEAWAYS

- Give the dark moments a time limit. Three days, not three years. Tell your brain the boundary.

- Not deciding is a decision. Drifting is a choice—and it always costs you.

- Pain isn't the problem. Avoidance is.

- Someone is watching how you handle your life. You're teaching them what resilience or cowardice looks like.

- You don't escape the dark night of the soul by thinking. You exit it by stepping forward—even when you're scared.

Asking For Help

Life can become overwhelming. There are moments when the weight feels unbearable and your mind tells you that escape is the only option.

If you ever experience true suicidal thoughts, please don't carry that alone. Ask for help.

If you're in the U.S.:
Call or text **988**—Suicide & Crisis Lifeline (24/7)
www.988lifeline.org

Outside the U.S.:
Visit **www.findahelpline.com** to find a trusted number in your country

If you feel in immediate danger, go to the nearest emergency room or contact local emergency services.

This book is not a substitute for professional mental health care.
Asking for help is not weakness, it's an act of self-respect.
Don't give up.

ACTION!

If you're ready to continue into the official third act of your hero's journey, block out 15 minutes and grab another blank card.

This next one isn't flashy.
It's not about solving your life.

It's about staying present long enough to realize what you must do next.

Fill out the card and get it up on your Director's Board.

Your dark night of the soul isn't permanent.
It's preparation.

You're still in the story.
You're in flux between your darkest hour and your brightest breakthrough.
You've earned your seat in the Director's chair.

Don't hand it back to your ego.

BEAT 12—THE BRIDGE

2:00 a.m. Questions

What thoughts keep circling when I can't sleep?

____

Am I *interested* in making my life better than any movie
or am I *committed*?

____

Who needs to see me step off the ledge and into the
challenge?

____

Memento Mori Declaration
Life is precious. I will persist in what matters most
because the alternative is...

____

____

____

ACT III
DiRECT YOUR LiFE

> "Success is the progressive
> realization of a worthy ideal."
> —Earl Nightingale

BEAT 13

YOU CALL THE SHOTS

"It's only after we've lost everything
that we're free to do anything."

—Tyler Durden, *Fight Club*

Fuck your ego!

Your ego loves to whisper: "I've learned enough. I'm good now."

This is when you need to hyper-focus on your commitment to growth.

You've cut through the noise, collected wisdom, taken hits, and picked yourself back up. That isn't victory—it's survival. Most people stop here, nodding along with books and podcasts, feeling inspired, and then never implementing a thing.

Don't let that little ego bastard hold you down. You deserve more.

Remember: knowledge acquisition makes you feel good, but knowledge implementation is when transformation happens.

I don't want you to just survive—I want you to thrive, handing out high-fives on the street because you're making progress and no longer afraid to "look dumb."

Get excited → Take action → Learn from success and failure → Gain confidence → Repeat.

That's how confidence compounds.
And the quality of your confidence is the quality of your life.

ROAD TRIP

The plan was simple: relocate to Cincinnati and manufacture opportunity.

Brandon had already shown me Cincinnati was night and day from L.A. I confirmed there was a growing film industry there.

My A Story met my B Story and for the first time in months, Act III had a map.

Karen and I packed my SUV to the brim—every possession we owned crammed inside like a Tetris champion's final boss.

We pulled away from Stephen's Malibu house. That view we'd grown used to. That constant reminder of what we'd built—and lost.

The ocean faded into the rear view mirror.

We hit the 101 Freeway, but this time I wasn't on that wall stealing in the dark.

I was road-tripping with my gorgeous wife. Adventuring.

We took about two weeks. I'll never understand why some people try to race across America in two sleepless days.

Yeahhh—no. We don't drink Red Bull and scarf down fast food.

Grand Canyon Views.
Wilderness.
New Mexico's Alien Town—she had to drag me away.
Hillbilly gas stations.
Roadside diners.

The move turned into our second honeymoon on wheels.

Then... hello, Cincinnati.

I pulled up to Brandon's duplex and did what any self-respecting Director would do—I blasted a ridiculous rap song called *"Scared Money"* so loud he could hear our arrival from inside.

I opened my door and started dancing in the driveway.
Brandon came out and joined me.
Way too long. Arms flailing. Terrible moves. Pure joy.

Karen sat in the passenger seat, caught somewhere between embarrassment and laughter. She probably was questioning every life choice that led her here.

This is what happens when you call your own shots.

You get to be ridiculous.
You get to celebrate.
You get to dance in driveways without caring who's watching.

That's freedom.

Freedom isn't drifting.
It's choosing a direction and committing to it.

I lost the house.
The safety net.
The proximity to "the industry."

And in losing all of it, I was finally free to build something entirely new.

THE THIRD ACT

In story structure, this moment is often called the Break Into Three.
It's where the hero stops surviving and starts executing.

Not because they gained new tools, but because they finally understand how to use the ones they already earned.

Everything clicks.
The debate ends.
The path forward becomes clear.

Think Neo in *The Matrix* realizing he IS the One.

Rocky getting the unconditional cheer from Adrian to win the fight.

Marty McFly in *Back to the Future* figuring out the exact moment his parents need to kiss at the dance.

Me, when I hit Cincinnati and realized confidence was portable.

The hero stops negotiating with fear, stops waiting for certainty, destroys doubt, and commits to the final showdown.

Within my first two years, I joined an acting agency and booked over twenty acting gigs—while simultaneously writing, coaching, and directing my own projects.

I created Custom Scene Creation: writing original scenes tailored to each actor, hiring professional crews, directing forty high-production-value scenes, and editing them into reels that looked like they were pulled straight from Hollywood.

We worked with over fifty actors. I created paid work for local crew members. Actors I coached gained clarity, booked more roles, and signed with larger agencies in bigger markets.

Forty scenes is essentially a feature film's worth of directed work—created while building my name in a brand-new city.

The local acting and film community knows my name now.

Not because I hoped.

Because I accepted my next call.
Because I created value.
Because I executed.

Years of trudging forward through wet sand, pushing through discomfort, and creating opportunities were far better than staying stuck as the shy guy full of self-pity.

The guy hovering at the food table at parties, pretending to be fascinated by the chips and dip instead of actually talking to anyone.

Low self-esteem dressed up as shyness. F.U.D. as my B.F.F. Always focused on me instead of being present with others.

That version of Tony is dead.
I killed him.

BREAKING THE PATTERN

Over the years, I've learned two powerful truths about intentionally placing myself in new physical environments:

It breaks limiting patterns.
It's exhilarating.

From my teens through adulthood, these shifts forced expansion in ways staying comfortable never could.

Each environment change wasn't about geography, it was about testing a deeper belief.

I could create opportunities anywhere.

Here's what a few of those shifts looked like across different chapters of my life:

Nashville:
My first real confidence breakthrough. I traveled solo to a packed karaoke bar and sang "Be-Bop-A-Lula"—terrifying, exhilarating, and completely out of my comfort zone. (Yes, I got a Queen request on a napkin from a silent beauty.)

New Orleans:

At a hostel during my introvert years, I actually befriended three girls and went out for ice cream and ghost tours.

For me, that was unheard of. It was the first time I felt my social confidence shifting.

Asia:

I felt like an alien on an alien planet. It forced me to connect in new ways—which, oddly, freed me.

Cincinnati:

With limited resources, I became resourceful.

Within six months, I connected with more people than I had in all my years growing up in Los Angeles.

Each environment shift forced me to stop retreating into ego and start directing my own experience.

Every move proved the same truth:
I can create value wherever I go.

Back in Beat 5, I warned you about the ORDINARY trap—the autopilot life most people never escape.

This is the opposite of that.

D.I.R.E.C.T.

To direct your life, you need an operating system. Here's one to memorize:

D–Don't overthink—*move*.
When your mind starts the "what if" spiral, cut it short. Action creates clarity, not the reverse.

I–Integrity over instant gratification

Every choice either builds or erodes your self-respect. Choose the path that makes you proud of who you're becoming.

R–Recite your reasons
Know why you're taking action. Your "why" becomes fuel when motivation fades.

E–Envision your target
See the outcome clearly—not only the goal, but how you'll feel achieving it.

C–Care for yourself deeply
You can't direct others or inspire confidence if you're running on empty.

T–Time is precious
Every moment you hesitate is a moment you can't get back. Act accordingly.

Read that again.

And before your ego jumps in, let me guess what it's saying:

"I've got a lot going on."

"I like my social media."

"Finding my *why* feels too personal-development-y."

"I don't have time for myself—I've got kids."

All of that might be true.
But here's the question I won't stop asking you:

Are you *interested* in making your life better than any movie—or are you *committed*?

Because interest waits.
Commitment moves.

And if not now, when?

I know what happens next. The enthusiasm fades. Life presses back.

Here's how to avoid the confidence crash once the initial motivation wears off. I want you to design the day where you feel clear, energized, and ready to take on anything, the kind of day you wish every day could feel like.

What has to happen for that day to exist?

If you can, block out two days this week.
Not to grind or escape.
But to give yourself the *perfect start* with no time limit.

Do the things you always say you'd do *if you had the time.*

But don't pick numbing vices.
Choose restorative fuel, the things that lift you up.

When your energy is up, do deep work on something that actually excites you.

You're tuning into the conditions that create your best days—on purpose. Once you know what fuels you most, narrow it down to three to five elements. Then compress the dose.

Shrink the feeling into 10–15 minutes you can deploy anytime.

Your brain and nervous system can be trained to shift into a powerful state with small bursts of output.

But first, you have to experience the *long version*.

Here's what that looks like.

Let's say you blast your favorite playlist and work out *or dance* for twenty minutes. Then you put on an empowering podcast and clean the house. Your body's moving, your space is reset, and you feel sharp. You rinse off, meet your best friend at a café, and plan an upcoming travel trip.

That's three and a half hours of a damn good start to your day.

You repeat a similar rhythm the next day—and actually book an airplane flight.

Then day three hits.

Responsibilities are back.

You've only got thirty minutes before real life storms in.

Here's the compressed dose.

You play one song.

You take a quick power walk.

You straighten one room.

You listen to fifteen minutes of the podcast.

You call your friend and share one new travel insight.

It's not the full experience and it doesn't need to be.

You're signaling the same triggers to your brain and nervous system.

Movement.

Music.

Connection.

Progress.

The message stays the same:

Life is good. I'm in motion. I'm in control.

That's how you carry the energy of your best days into your busiest ones.

Here's one obnoxiously long example, not a prescription.

My personal power routine (morning):

- 24 ounces of water with lemon, apple cider vinegar

- Wash face, brush teeth with the opposite hand to activate the brain

- Make ridiculous faces in the mirror—force a smile

- Smother my wife with kisses once I'm fully awake—or else I'm a groggy jerk (oxytocin)

- Sunlight + reading with Bulletproof coffee (serotonin + dopamine)

- Stretch and light workout (serotonin + endorphins)

- Solve my Rubik's Cube (dopamine)

- Cold shower for 2–3 minutes with breathwork—make silly noises like a kid (endorphins + dopamine)

- Then get to my life's work

When I activate this, people think:

"This guy's weird. Where does he get his energy? What happened to him?"

The goal isn't to copy my routine.

It's to discover what makes you feel unstoppable, then compress it into ten minutes.

This lines up with what Josh Waitzkin talks about in his book *The Art of Learning*: building condensed rituals that trigger peak performance. He calls it shortening the recovery time. I call it momentum protection.

Because when you can recreate your best state on demand, momentum never leaves you.

"Hope and fear are both phantoms
that arise from thinking of the self.
When we don't see the self *as
self*, what do we have to fear?"

—Lao Tzu, *Tao Te Ching* (Stephen Mitchell)

CONFIDENCE IS CONTAGIOUS

Think about the people in your life: friends, family, even strangers. When you step into confidence, when you own your presence, you give others permission to do the same.

Confidence isn't magic, it's a skill. Practice it, improve it, and your entire life improves.

Sometimes you literally have to pick yourself up—physically—and put yourself in new situations. Even standing in front of your Director's board, mapping your story beats, is uncomfortable for some people. But that's where growth starts.

On the other side of uncomfortable action is everything you want.

Playfulness is the path. Curiosity is the compass.

Take action and confidence will be the outcome.

You deserve to feel your best, tap into your authentic self, create a compelling vision for your future, and live in the moment with joyous kid-like vigor no matter what.

In fact, it's your job now.
You're hired!

Once you do this, you uncover the clouds that were fogging your playful heart. That's when you rediscover the magic you always had inside.

You're the Director now.

The question isn't whether you're ready—it's which scene you'll shoot first.

DIRECTOR'S COMMENTARY

You've been through the wild west: wrangled chaos, survived a few saloon brawls, and lived long enough to witness the beginning of your own transformation.

Sounds exaggerated? Good. Exaggeration is what makes cartoons work.

And if you don't appreciate cartoons... I don't know how you made it this far in the book.

By now, you know what Act III is for. This is where theory becomes action. and knowledge turns into implementation. Where you stop being the student and become the mad scientist in the Director's hat.

The camera is rolling and your life *is* the movie.
You're not waiting for someone else to call "Action."
You are the action.

Which means it's time to show up for the final showdown.

KEY TAKEAWAYS

- The new information: You can create opportunities anywhere
- Ego exposed: Low self-esteem is ego focused on me instead of presence
- Confidence is a skill: Practice it, compress it, make it contagious
- The Director's Loop: Excitement → Action → Learning → Confidence → Repeat
- Say it out loud: Limiting beliefs collapse when spoken—use that
- Break the pattern: Environment shifts test and strengthen new beliefs

ACTION!

This isn't about being naturally talented. I don't buy that myth. It's about cultivated enthusiasm and deliberate effort. You build what you believe in.

Think of billiards. You call the shot before you take it. You name it, commit to it, then sink it with conviction. That's the energy I want from you here.

Fill out this pivotal card and get it on your Director's Board.

BEAT 14

LOCK THE CUT

"I have a perfect cure for a sore throat: cut it."

—Alfred Hitchcock

It feels good when you don't overreact.

The other morning, I was heading out for a job when I got in my car, and something felt *off*.

DING DING DING DING DING.

I *heard* the ignition key sound, but I hadn't put the key in yet.

The car was a mess.
There was a luggage rack key from my glove box crammed into the ignition, like someone had tried to start the car.

My car had been broken into.

Someone tried to steal from me and messed with my life.
They nervously jammed my roof luggage key into the ignition.
It was obvious it wouldn't fit but they went for it anyway and got it stuck.

I was about to be pissed, but then I *spotted the scene.*

Someone was desperate.

That was the best they could do with the information, emotion, and love they did—or didn't—have.

I felt sorry more than anything.
I could feel the remnants of a tattered soul.

I had to *cut this scene* out of my day so I could *have* a day.

My car was still there.
No major damage done.

I cleaned up the mess, pried the wrong key out, and put the right key in the ignition.

Then I made a couple of *edits to my day*:

Keep my car in my backyard instead of on the street from now on. Shift my focus to my daily priorities. Finally, I consciously *locked the decision* to move on to the next moments waiting for me.

I completely forgot about the whole scene until I sat down to share it here.

Why?

I tapped into equanimity, magnanimity, and perseverance.
Good thing I got my power routine in beforehand and didn't go on a rabid rampage against the degenerates of society like the old days.

My heart didn't skip a beat.
I didn't call my wife in a panic.

I made what I call a *Soul Cut.*

THE SOUL CUT™ METHOD

This is the very concept that took me off that freeway wall back in Beat 1 and into my own hero's journey.

It can be activated in huge, life-altering moments or in the small, pesky ones that quietly screw up your day.

Either way, it's the quintessential action-packed sequence that allows you to direct your life.

The ideal outcome:

- Create a clear vision of what matters to you
- Break through your barriers
- Rediscover your magic
- Give back—from overflow, not obligation
- Make your life better than any movie

The prerequisite:

- Hyper-awareness—which you've been building through Beats 1–13
- Care for your life more
- Intentionally make a Soul Cut

Regardless of your faith or belief system, I'll be using the word *soul* to emphasize your life force—your energy, your essence, the highest version of you.

Think of your soul like an invisible cape you were born with.

It was designed to help you fly.

In childhood, it collected the beautiful things—dreams, love, wonder, questions, excitement, courage, and that natural curiosity that made everything feel possible.

For some, abuse disrupted that collection early.
But for most of us, the cape began as pure magic.

Then we entered the overcrowded world.

Every fall.
Every disappointment.
Every "you're too much," "not enough," "stupid," "fat," "ugly," or "weird" got tangled into those original gifts.

The beautiful things are still there: dreams, love, ideas, kindness, freedom, courage.

But they get buried under layers of F.U.D.—Fear, Uncertainty, Doubt.

Over time, the cape gets heavy.

You can't fly when your cape is weighed down by debris and filth. You can't even leave the ground if someone is stepping on it while dumping their negative footage all over it.

The Soul Cut is the moment you look at the reel of your past and the reel of your present—then start slicing with a razor.

- I'm keeping the lessons.
- I'm cutting the weight.

This is where everything you've immersed yourself in so far comes together into four decisive stages.

1. Spot the Scene (Awareness)

See the loop you're in—name the scene.
"This is the 'I'm not enough' scene"—or the "this is good, but I want better" scene. The moment you name it, you're no longer trapped inside it.

You're directing it.

2. Cut the F.U.D. (Fear, Uncertainty, Doubt)

Trim anything adding drag to your cape: toxic inputs, leaky boundaries, numbing habits, stale identities, complacency.

Cutting isn't cruelty.
It's clarity.

3. Edit for Truth (Reframe)

Swap the lie for what's real and useful.
"I failed" → "I learned."
"They left" → "That chapter ended."

Meaning replaces victimhood.

4. Lock the Cut (Commit)

Choose the new behavior or identity and live it.
No more re-editing the same scene.

"I am someone who sets boundaries and makes decisions without guilt."

Lock it. Roll the next scene.

Spot → Cut → Edit → Lock.

Let's expand this framework so you can apply, ingrain, and condition it into your own hero's journey.

SPOT THE SCENE

Awareness is the Director's most powerful tool.
You can't edit what you can't see.

This step is about recognizing the scene you're in—the emotional pattern, story loop, or behavior that keeps replaying.

What role, belief, or identity doesn't belong?
What bad scene are you stuck in?

When I was twenty-five, I was stuck in a scene where I didn't belong *anywhere*.

I believed my art—*my worth*—would only be recognized after I died.
I believed I'd never experience true love again.

I finally snapped into awareness while living in that warehouse I mentioned in Beat 7.

One of my *10 roommates*—Pam, with a heart of gold—gently grabbed my hand and *started reading my palm*.

I wasn't sure what she was doing at first.
When it clicked, my inner skeptic kicked in: *"Do I humor this... or pull my hand back?"*

Then she looked up with her friendly face and said:

"Tony, you're so afraid the world won't understand you that you're not letting anyone understand you."

Seeing myself through her honest eyes pulled me out of the scene I was hiding in.

My eyes teared up.

This is where *you* become the observer of your own life.

You step back from the chaos and look closer:

What story am I reliving right now and is it worth keeping in my final cut?
What emotions keep showing up uninvited?
What limiting belief is running this scene?

Like a director watching playback, you have to see it before you can adjust it.

Most people never spot the scene.
They keep acting in it, wondering why life feels like a bad sequel.

When you feel triggered, pause.
Slow your reaction.

Awareness breaks the loop.

CUT THE F.U.D.

Every great editor trims what slows down the story.
Same in life.

You need to cut the internal noise and external distractions that drag you down.

This step is incredibly difficult—because it requires courage.
And I know firsthand how often courage gets confused with the confidence paradox:

When I'm confident, then I'll do the thing.

It's the opposite.

Courage isn't about having no fear—it's about stepping forward anyway.
And when you work this muscle long enough, you don't need to flex.

That same week Pam read my palm, I made a huge Soul Cut.

Somewhere between listening to Earl Nightingale—one of the original voices of modern personal development—and Pam's palm reading, I made a declaration.

Out loud. To myself. And to others.

I had spent a decade cycling through intermittent depression, negativity, and angst.
Now it was time to do the opposite.

I decided—out of curiosity and experimentation—to see what it was like to *join the force.*

To get uncomfortable.
To move forward anyway.

Cutting isn't about removing.
It's about letting go, setting boundaries, and sometimes bleeding.

Remember, F.U.D. is your brain's ancient alarm system trying to keep you "safe."
But safe often means sad—and stuck.

What's adding drag to your life?
What can you cut today?

Maybe it's:

- The energy vampire that drains you
- The job that kills your soul
- The habit that numbs instead of heals
- The limiting belief that slaps you with, *"you're not ready"*
- The people-pleasing pattern that robs you of caring for yourself

This isn't about being cold or cruel.
It's about recognizing what no longer serves your growth and having the courage to let it go.

Sometimes cutting F.U.D. means having a hard conversation. Sometimes it means walking away quietly.
Sometimes it means saying no when you've always said yes.

Identify what you're tolerating that's weighing down your cape.

What would the Director of your life do about this?

Then do that thing—this week.

It may hurt.
You might bleed.

But that's the price of transformation.

EDIT FOR TRUTH

When a scene isn't working, Directors don't quit.
They change the angle, lens, lighting—and like in *Back to the Future*, they even replaced the lead actor mid-production and reshot the film. That decision saved the movie.

In life, reframing turns pain into wisdom.
It's where "Why me?" becomes "What's this teaching me?"

This is where meaning replaces victimhood.
Don't be the victim.
Be the victor.

If you've seen me work on a film set or speak on stage, you'd probably think:
Tony's outgoing, social, confident, and kinda dorky.

But up until Pam's palm reading—and that specific Soul Cut—I was so in my head *I was dead.*

I was deeply attached to my loner, woe-is-me identity.
And because of that, I was missing the magic in life.

To change that, I had to fully immerse myself in positive psychology books, courses, events, places, and people—the exact things the old me would've scoffed at and judged.

I had to do things that made me uncomfortable to make the shift:

Smiling at people.
Shaking hands.
Hugging people.

I remember two moments that helped me start editing for truth.

While visiting my older sister in college, she said:
"Tone, you don't know how to hug."

Later, a love interest—after hugging a friend goodbye for summer break—said:
"I didn't hug you because I know you don't like hugs."

I remember, embarrassingly, saying,
"What do you mean?"

I was my own *oxytocin robber.*
Oxytocin is the connection chemical—released when we bond, hug, trust, and feel close to another human.

Those were hyper-awareness moments.
They forced me to rethink my overthinking comfort zone—and how I was actually living.

Was that the real me?
A non-hugger who's awkward all the time?

Or was that a *made-up me*—built from too many stacked, historic, catastrophic moments blown wildly out of proportion?

Here's the aha:

After a lot of effort—surrounding myself with quality people, quality content, and quality self-growth—I stayed in long enough.

You gotta stay in long enough.

That's when I developed what psychologists call self-efficacy and self-agency:

- *I believe I can do this.*
- *I am the Director of my life.*

I'm now a master hugger, if you're curious.

And by the way, if you're not a hugger, I'm calling you out. That's not okay. You need oxytocin as part of a healthy life. So get over it and get into it—specifically a 30-second hold, which is when the connection effect actually kicks in.

This has been researched and tested... sooooo yeah.
Hug me when you see me.

Editing for truth means replacing the lie you've been believing with what you actually want.

In my case, I needed deeper connection. I had to edit those elements into my life to uncover that truth.

Add humor.
Find the lesson.
Discover the gift in the garbage.

The lie: "I'm not good enough."
The truth: "I'm still learning, and that's exactly where I should be."

The lie: "Everyone leaves me."
The truth: "Some people weren't meant for my next scene, and that's fine."

The lie: "I wasted all that time."
The truth: "Every detour taught me something I needed to know."

Reframing isn't toxic positivity.
It's choosing a lens that empowers instead of paralyzes.

Take the scene you spotted earlier and reframe it.

Old story: "I failed again. I'm not cut out for this."
New story: "I got feedback. Now I know what doesn't work. I'm one step closer. Take action."

Write it down.
Say it out loud.
Make it your new script.

LOCK THE CUT

Once you lock picture with your editor, there's no more tweaking.
Some film Directors—me included—stay hands-on for final touches, but eventually you have to declare it done.

In your life, this means choosing the new identity, behavior, or belief and living it out.
You must leave the old self behind to move forward.

No more re-edits. No second-guessing.
Lock the decision. Then keep refining the life.

This is where you decide: "This is my life—and I'm the Director."

You don't just think the new thought.

You act from it.
You don't just reframe the story.
You live the reframe.

Locking the cut is a decision.
A line in the sand.

Then make it real—tell someone you trust, write it down on your wall, create the triggers that keep you from slipping back.

Once I got a taste of my new and improved identity, I never wanted to go back to my old one. That's not to say I didn't slip here and there—but I was always able to climb back out because I stopped being *interested* and started *committing*.

I stopped being bitter.
I started being better.

When the sour crabs tried to yank me back as I shared my new self, I had to shake them off.

When I used new vocabulary and was ridiculed—literally—I had to say: *Don't condemn me for my pursuit of improvement.*

When loved ones rolled their eyes, I had to roll out new patience.

Make your decision—and cut everything else off.

When old patterns creep back in—and they will—remind yourself: *"That scene is cut. I'm not running that footage anymore."*

I know that can feel impossible.
But that's usually because you're *in* the forest—not outside it.

Sometimes you need to dissociate.
Watch the movie of your life from the edit bay.
Instruct the editor (yourself) what to cut, what to keep, and how to reframe it.
Then sit back, experience it again, and adjust.

That's how you reach your final cut.

The key is distance.
When you can watch the pain without reliving it, you become both artist and audience.

That's when the Soul Cut becomes healing—not just editing.

> "If we fail to focus on the story
> of our lives, we become bit
> players in other people's stories.
> Playing the director of our own movie
> gives us the ability to choose our
> entire character and life's arc."
>
> —Brendon Burchard, *The Motivation Manifesto*

We Have Good Scenes And Bad Scenes

You've shot more scenes than you can count for your *life-movie.*

You've captured transformations—the moments of breakdown and breakthrough—the evidence that you can direct your life.

Some scenes are brilliant.
Some are boring.
Most are somewhere in between.

Every filmmaker knows this scene: you're alone in the edit bay at midnight, staring at hundreds of hours of footage trying to find the story.

Like an editor, your job isn't to use every piece of footage, it's to select the pieces that serve the story you're trying to tell.

Phenomenal films are made in the edit.

You can have Academy Award-winning performances, gorgeous cinematography, and powerful scenes, but if you can't assemble them into a coherent story that moves the audience, you've got nothing but expensive footage.

The same is true for your life.

All the insights, experiments, and growth moments you've created need to be edited into a sustainable system.
Otherwise, you'll get lost in miles of raw footage with no story.

In film, the finale is where the hero faces the final test—proving they've absorbed every lesson from Act II.

The dragon gets slayed.
The quest is won.
The smoke clears and the hero has transformed.

Their fatal flaw?
Repaired.
The world?
A better place because they showed up.

That's where you are now.

You've been through the pressure cooker, survived the collapse, and walked through your dark night. You've gathered your crew, expanded your map, and called the shots.

Now it's time to lock your cut and *project* who you are—before some uncreative studio executive edits *your movie.*

Your job as Director is to select the practices, habits, and systems that serve the life you're trying to create.

So how do you know what to keep and what to cut?

THE DIRECTOR'S SACRED WINDOW

Here's what you need to understand: protecting and directing the first 30–60 minutes of your day—before anyone breaches your space—is the tiny time window that determines everything.

Miss it, and you're reacting to everyone else's script notes instead of writing your own.

You lose your entire day when you wake up and immediately check your phone, answer emails, or consume whatever nonsense is thrown in your face.

Next thing you know, hours have passed, and you're in a bad mood—too drained to even think about what you want your life to be about.

That's not directing.
That's drifting with a job title.

The most successful people I know—across every industry—guard their morning like it's the only take they'll get. Because in many ways, it is. How you spend your first hour sets the tone, energy, and focus for everything that follows.

When I conquer my morning, no bad news can penetrate and deflate my force field. I still have empathy and feel, but I don't let it consume my entire day.

Remember *Recte Vivere*—to live rightly?
I focus my camera on doing the right thing as often as possible.

It's about priming yourself in the morning so you're in a strong state—before the world makes demands, before the chaos starts, before you're needed by everyone else. In Beat 13, I shared my morning routine. But I didn't tell you why it matters so much. That routine isn't only about feeling good. It's about maintaining directorial control over my state, my focus, and my decisions.

When I skip it, I notice immediately.
I'm reactive instead of proactive.
I'm an irritable jerk instead of a centered gentleman.
I make half-ass decisions from a low-energy state instead of defining ones from a peak state.

That's the difference between directing your life and being directed.

And when you protect your sacred window, you can take out the razor blade and start cutting intentionally.

SELF-MASTERY VS. SELF-DISCIPLINE

Do not confuse self-discipline with self-mastery. They're not the same thing.

Self-discipline is doing what keeps you functioning even when you don't feel like it: brushing your teeth, paying bills, showing up to work, staying in shape, calling family to stay connected.

It's your baseline.

Self-mastery is deeper. It's the healthy obsession to expand your being because you understand this life is a gift and you refuse to waste it.

It's pushing your limits physically, mentally, and spiritually.
It's staying grounded when things go sideways.

It's why I decided to write this book—not only to solidify these lessons for you, but to see who I become in the process.

Part of self-mastery is learning to love yourself the way a great parent loves a child—with standards, patience, and support.

Only then do you begin to treat your time with real respect. And when you value your time, you start using it with intention.

Self-mastery means committing to constant and never-ending improvement.

You'll never get it perfect, and you don't need to.
Progress is enough.

DIRECTOR'S COMMENTARY

When you make the necessary Soul Cuts, your life is simply better.

It creates space to prioritize what actually matters instead of speeding on the freeway internally screaming, *"Move it, asshole—I have no time!"*

I've never done that, by the way.

Okay—maybe one memorable stint of road rage in my twenties in Los Angeles. You'll have to ask me about that in person.

The real idea here is simple: transformation has to become integration.

You want it ingrained. Automatic. A habitual internal check:

Does this serve me?
Does this serve me anymore?
Who do I want to be today?
What should I be doing more of? Less of?
What can I control—and what can I let go of?

Directing your life isn't about filming a million takes.
It's about cutting wisely.

Create practices that serve your story.
Build simple systems that survive stress.
Track progression, not perfection.

I believe each year we get the chance to lock the cut on a beautiful movie.
Months are your acts. Weeks are your scenes. Days are your takes. If you're
lucky enough to have another year, use it to refine your story.

Not perfection. Progress.

The real test is this:

Can you maintain your transformation when life gets chaotic?
Can you keep cutting the noise and locking in what matters?

Because every edit shapes the story.
Make yours worth living, watching, and rewatching.

KEY TAKEAWAYS

- Films are made in the edit. So is your life. Raw footage ≠ finished story.
- Guard your opening hour. Lose the morning, lose the movie.
- Self-mastery > self-discipline. Discipline maintains. Mastery expands.
- Soul Cut = Spot → Cut → Edit → Lock. Four decisive moves. Repeat as needed.
- Don't prove it. *Project it.*

ACTION!

I want you to cut your soul.

I know—that sounds like something ripped from the film *American Psycho*, but I'm not being edgy for effect.

This is your moment to walk into the edit room, sit in the chair, and lock it all in.

No more rewrites on this decision.
No more hoarding footage.
This is where intention becomes identity.

Make your cut.

Be sure to take your time with this one.
Enjoy editing your life-movie.

Pin it to your Director's Board.

This is your finale—for whichever section of your life you're working on.
Lock the cut.

You're now carrying the ultimate boon.
The reward you started this journey for.
One beat left.

Time to meet the new you.

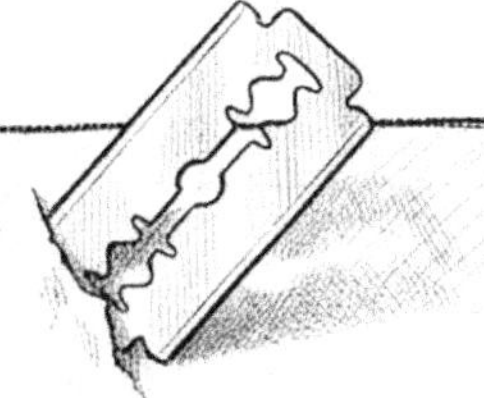

BEAT 14—MY SOUL CUT

Spot
What bad scene am I stuck in?

____

____

Cut
What needs to be removed? No negotiations.

____

Edit
What truth, belief, or behavior gets edited in?
(Trim what doesn't serve. Reframe what does.)

____

____

Lock
How do I lock the cut—what action makes it real?

____

____

BEAT 15

YOU ARE THE REWARD

"The cave you fear to enter holds the treasure you seek."

—Joseph Campbell

This is your *after* photo. Proof of how far
you and your inner world have traveled.

In film, the Final Image mirrors the Opening Image and reveals the distance traveled. My Opening Image was a self-loathing nihilist caught in negative cycles. The Final Image is someone who responds with presence instead of panic and treats challenges as adventures instead of threats—one person, new operating system. I learned to direct my life instead of letting circumstances and bitterness direct me.

I'm now the one who initiates family Zoom calls.
I perform magic for my sister's kids to connect.
I call my dad and push past small talk.
I choose patience over distance.
When I'm a jerk, I catch it fast and apologize.

I'm sharing this for one reason: *transformation is possible.*

If you stayed with this process, you're not the same person who started it. You've been expanding your being the entire time, whether you felt it or not.

It's your turn to look at the distance you've traveled.

Who were you when you started this book?

What fears were driving you?

What story were you telling yourself about what was possible?

And who are you now?

Not perfect—but different.

Not finished—but evolved.

That gap between those two versions of you is proof.

If the only thing you walk away with is the habit of responding instead of reacting, you've already made real progress. The ability to pause, shake your head at the chaos, and even laugh when life doesn't go your way is a skill every Director must master. You now have the awareness, the questions, and the tools to practice it.

It's not about having all the answers.

It's about having agency.

The power to choose your response.

The courage to embrace the Director role.

The discipline to course-correct without self-betrayal.

And when F.U.D. creeps in, measure yourself by this upgraded definition of success:

The progressive realization of a worthy ideal, paired with the willingness to stay *playful* while pursuing it.

Not rigid. Not joyless. Not heavy. *Playful.* That's what keeps you curious. Curiosity keeps you moving. Movement builds confidence—and that loop doesn't have to end.

Transformation is proven in the next crisis. It's revealed in how you respond when things wobble again.

And there will be wobbling.

I don't know what yours will be, but now you have something you didn't before:

Evidence that you can handle more than you thought.
Freedom to expand.
Trust in yourself.

"Every man dies.
Not every man really lives."

—William Wallace, *Braveheart*

If this were your final image, would you be proud of how you showed up?

Start forming the closing frame for every area that matters: your relationships, your health, your career, your character, your contribution.

You were born to express your best self.

Don't let fear, temporary comfort, or other people's opinions steal the Director's chair from you again.

And don't forget to have fun.

Because every story that matters ends the same way.
In every hero's journey, the hero returns home with a gift.

Not what they found.
Who they became.

Your story was the training.
Who you became is the gift.

The world needs more Directors—people who stop the reruns and take responsibility for creating the life they want instead of waiting to be rescued.

You are one of them now.

DIRECTOR'S COMMENTARY

This isn't an ending. It's your launch pad.

I'm not there with you physically, but I know you've put a lot of work into your life. I know you—and everyone else—have a compelling life-movie inside, waiting to be made.

You didn't go through the 15 beats.
You reflected on your own story.

Every beat asked you to examine your life, make real choices, and plot a personal transformation.

That's the work, and it matters.

Here's what I share with my actors:

"As long as you pick a direction for your character and *commit* to it, you've done your job. Just remember, the scene is malleable. You must adapt when it's not working."

Progress over perfection.

Don't wait until you feel ready.
You're ready the moment you call action.

If you stayed present through this journey, you're living proof that internal transformation is real.

You're more aligned with what you actually care about.
And when that alignment happens, service becomes natural.

Confidence becomes quiet.
Direction becomes obvious.

As long as you integrate what resonated into your identity, you'll create a life you're excited to live.

On set, film directors review their scenes daily.
You can do the same.

Ask yourself:

Did I play big today?
Did I stay curious like a kid?
Did I course-correct when I drifted?

You have infinite room to expand your map.
You can go further than you think.
You are capable of loving more deeply than you've allowed yourself to believe.

Directors don't always know if the next scene will work.
They show up.
They call action.
They adjust in real time.

That's your job now too.

KEY TAKEAWAYS

- Transformation shows up in the Final Image.

- Real change is internal, integrated, and contagious. Others feel it before you explain it.

- The true test is how you respond to the next disruption.

- You get to define the closing frame for every area that matters.

- You were born to become your best self. Start directing from that truth.

ACTION!

You're near the finish line.

This is where F.U.D. gets loud—throwing distractions, doubts, and last-minute excuses.

Stay steady.
Stay committed.
Stay in your own race.

Grab your final index card.
Complete it and proudly pin it in the last position on your Director's Board.

This is your Academy Award moment.

BEAT 15—MY REWARD

Final Image
What does my life look like now?
Without overthinking, what tells me I've changed?

____

Proof
What specific action proves I'm not who I was?

____

New Default
How do I respond to challenge now?

____

Service
Who benefits because I showed up and grew?

____

Next Move
What am I directing next?

____

Take a deep breath in through your nose.
Exhale out your mouth, twice as long.

This is where you slow down and revel in your work.

Read all fifteen beat cards from start to finish.
Notice the full arc of your transformation.
Let it land.

You just did something rare.
You stayed committed long enough for change to happen.
That's how progress is made.

If you completed all 15 beats, you *integrated the work*.

If you hesitated or skipped parts, that's okay. You're not behind.
But don't stop here.

Remember this:

You are not your past behavior.
You are who you choose to become again and again.

Your life-movie is always rolling.
Still yours to direct.

You are the reward.
Now go live like it.

YOUR MARK

Building your Director's Board through Beat 15 if proof you're willing to do what most people never do.

Commit.

If you want to mark this moment:

- Snap a photo of your completed Director's Board
- Share it
- Tag me **@TonySuriano**

Not for validation.

For evidence—to yourself—that you followed through.

I'll be featuring completed boards as inspiration at **directyourlifebook.com**.

Real people.

Real decisions.

Real progress.

Title:
Logline:

Reality | Theme | World | Wake-Up Call | F.U.D.

All In | Connection | Expansion | Reversal | Pressure

Collapse | Bridge | Shot Caller | Soul Cut | Reward

PiCTURES UP

"Inaction breeds doubt and fear.
Action breeds confidence and courage."

—Dale Carnegie

It's funny—life always seems to hand
you the next reversal right after a reward.

But when you live as a Director, you stop seeing that as punishment.

It's how you stay awake.
It's how you keep from drifting and *keep it fun.*

You find a new angle.
You look through a different lens.
And you go again.

That's the exact mindset I was in when it happened.

I'm driving through Cincinnati, my mind hyper-focused *and scattered* at the same time: on this book, the stage performances I'm manifesting, potential film gigs, the ways I can continue building a life better than any movie. I'm thinking about how to contribute more to my family and the world… while also in the middle of decisions that would shape the next decade of my life—depending on whether I doubled down on the risk or quietly retreated from it.

Yet I'm centered.
Good thing I had my morning power routine.

Then my phone lights up—KareBear calling.

Normally, my phone is on Do Not Disturb. Sacred thinking time.
But today, for whatever reason, it's off.

I answer.

"You're going to be daddy Tony," she blurts out.

I don't react immediately. I let it sink in—life-changing information arriving mid-scene.

"Hm… are you sure?" I ask, trying not to be fazed.

"There are two lines. I'm pregnant!"

Then it hits me.

I fumble my words. I urge her to take a second test while we're on the phone. This time, it's undeniable.

A thought flashes through my mind:
Is this really the right time? I thought I'd be further along with… everything.

Then I catch myself.

That was the old pattern trying to sneak back in.
This was my new call. Literally.

So I decide. Fast.
I accept it.
I choose adventure.
I love it.
Amor fati.

And in that moment, driving through Cincinnati with life-altering news in my ear, I realize I've come a long way from the guy balancing on a freeway wall, stealing in the shadows, hating the world and the people in it.

I used to snarl,
"I would never bring a child into this messed-up world."

And now, soon, I'll be saying,
"Welcome to this beautiful world," to my own.

I arrive home and show KareBear the best version of myself I can summon. Together, we process the news with joy, disbelief, laughter, and the awe that follows something real. Looking back at my early twenties—never believing I was capable of intimacy, marriage, or deserving love—this version of me feels almost unreal. Not because life got easier, but because I learned how to meet it differently.

And with this final image for *this film*, the next feature is already greenlit.

It premieres in nine months at my own house.
The script is written in diapers and midnight cries.
Directed with unconditional love.

That's the one I'll be directing for the rest of my life.

FINAL FRAME

By now, you've met your life differently too

You realize that the quality of your confidence *is* the quality of your life. It determines how you show up in your relationships, your work, and with yourself.

If research shows us anything, it's this: to make your life better than any movie, you must build the skill the happiest and most fulfilled people cultivate—confidence.

Confidence grows when you learn new and meaningful things.
When you build an identity rooted in self-trust.
When you choose connection over isolation.
When you give yourself credit for what you've accomplished.

Like finishing this book.

And you didn't just read a book.
You gathered evidence.

Evidence that you can stay present when things shake, choose direction instead of drift, and adapt without abandoning yourself.

This isn't theory anymore.
It's yours.

When you feel stuck, overwhelmed, or complacent, you know where to return—to the work, to the questions, to the role you've chosen.

This is how you keep directing.

Too many people die without ever crafting their life-movie.
Don't be one of them.

Direct your life *or someone else will.*

Here *you* go.
Pictures up.

THE DIRECTOR'S BOARD

HERO CARD

Title—What are you calling this season of your life?

Logline—In one sentence, who are you becoming?

THE 15 BEATS

1. Reality—See your life clearly. No distortion.
2. Heart of the Story—Decide what your life stands for.
3. Your World—Audit your environment and influences.
4. Wake-Up Call—Recognize the invitation to grow.
5. Face F.U.D.—Say yes despite fear, uncertainty, and doubt.
6. All In—Commit. No half-measures.
7. Connection—Build your cast and crew intentionally.
8. Expansion—Update your map through lived experience.
9. Reversal—Who are you when the proof disappears?
10. Pressure—Train steadiness when everything shakes.
11. Collapse—Let the old version of you fall away.
12. Bridge—Stop drifting. Step forward before you feel ready.
13. Shot Caller—Own your choices without apology.
14. Soul Cut—Spot → Cut → Edit → Lock.
15. Reward—Become the proof of your own transformation.

REVIEW REQUEST

DIRECTOR TO DIRECTOR

Thank you for reading *Direct Your Life*.

If this book gave you the energy to take action on what matters—*and have more fun doing it*—I'd love for you to leave a short review.

Leaving a short review does two things:

1. It creates a small moment of human connection—giving and receiving, which genuinely feels good for both of us.

2. It signals to the platforms that this book matters. Reviews trigger the algorithm to share it with more people who need it—so your few sentences could help someone else start directing their life too.

You can leave an honest review here:

directyourlifebook.com/review

I read every review to understand what's landing and who this work is helping.

Thank you for committing.
Thank you for staying in long enough.
And thank you for helping this message reach the next person who needs it.

Tony

**Get more resources and continue the work at
DirectYourLifeBook.com/Continue**

THE DAILY DIRECTION SYSTEM

This is where Directors recalibrate daily.

I created a free 1-page tool to direct each day with clarity, identity, and momentum.

Serious about directing your life? Direct your day.

THE PODCAST

For when you need your posture reset.

Real stories. Hard truths. Philosophy applied.
A jolt of perspective when drift tries to creep back in.

This is where Directors return when comfort starts whispering.

THE MASTERMIND

This is the room.

Live sessions. Real accountability. No spectators.
A private space for those done negotiating with fear, ego, and F.U.D.

Directors do not build alone forever.
They sharpen each other.
If you're ready for expansion—not information—this is your next cut.

MEET THE AUTHOR

TONY SURIANO is a film director, keynote speaker, and recovering nihilist who believes your life is either a movie worth watching—or a rerun nobody asked for.

In his twenties, Tony was a lost nomad—shy and restless, stuck in cycles of doubt. Today, he has directed more than eighty projects for brands including Head & Shoulders and the European Space Agency, appeared in The Irishman under Martin Scorsese alongside Robert De Niro and Joe Pesci, and coached hundreds of creatives to stop drifting and start directing.

Growing up in Hollywood, Tony watched powerful moguls achieve everything and still feel empty. After decades studying filmmaking and human behavior—and training under leaders like Tony Robbins and Brendon Burchard—he recognized something simple but powerful: the same 15-beat story structure behind billion-dollar films can reshape real lives. That insight became the Director's Board™—a practical framework for turning awareness into action.

Tony pursues challenges that sharpen focus and test commitment: solving a Rubik's Cube in twenty-six seconds, unicycling down stairs, building a house in Malibu with his bare hands, motorcycling solo across America, hopping freight trains, and traveling throughout Asia for nine months. On one occasion, that obsession even got him kicked out of a circus for attempting to unionize jugglers.

He's on a crusade to stop people from drifting so they can make their lives better than any movie.

Tony lives in Ohio with his wife and their child, continuing to conjure up new challenges worth taking on.

END CREDiTS

Every Director knows a project is never made alone.

To my family, friends, mentors, and coaches—the ones who said:

"Try it"
"Don't think too much"
"I love you no matter what"
"You're going to do great things."
"I believe in you."
"Keep going."
"You're stronger than you think."
"Live. Love. Matter."
"Only compare yourself to yourself yesterday."
"Change it, accept it, or leave it."
"Ask better questions."
"Never dim your light."
"The biggest risk in life is not taking one."

Family

To my parents—for your creative support, your black sheep mindset, and for raising a kid who asked way too many questions.

To my sisters—for always having my back.

To my godfather—for teaching me that authenticity is power.

And to my spirited wife, Karen, A.K.A. "KareBear"—who transformed my life by holding me accountable, raising my standards, and choosing adventure when comfort was easier.

And to our soon to be baby, "Coco"—I love you, I'm excited for you, and I thank you for being the new fire under my ass.

I'd quite literally be living on the streets—or worse, stuck in a life directed by everyone but me—if it weren't for all of *you*.

Cast & Crew

Daniel Aceves, A.K.A. "Danny Legs"—for being my intellectual bounce board and saving me in a moment of desperation.

Sacha Riviere—for your mentorship and continuous support.

Chad Nelson—for yelling, "You're going to be in this movie!" when I needed it most.

Brandon Estrada—for our skateboard sessions. For opening Cincinnati to me when L.A. closed its doors.

Shane Edele & Cyrus Wymer—the silly duo: for always being there for me and making me laugh.

Armen Pogosyan—for always being up for adventure.

Marcus Perea—for the hilariously fast, radically open conversations that gave me breaks from my work.

Gary Serino—for being the peaceful bridge.

David Phillippi—for your generosity, mentorship, friendship, and magic.

Sam Wright & Laura VonHolle—for welcoming me into your lives.

JJ Bernold—for seeing me through the ups and downs and still rooting for me.

Christina Montanez—for your kind-hearted spirit.

Stephen Polk—for taking my wife and me in when we were down on our luck.

Antonio Goodwin (Kyo Sa Nim)—for teaching me that my limits are my lies.

Mr. Kelly—for your film class and the encouragement that started me out.

Mrs. Rogers—for pulling me aside after class and telling me I'm a writer.

Dr. Maroul Russell—for asking, "What if you didn't have to worry about everyone else?" and changing how I show up for myself.

Jessa Fontelo—for being my bridge to the Philippines.

Karl Fehringer—for being my guide through the Philippines.

Patrick Langley—for the conversations and camaraderie in the Philippines.

Pam Cash—for randomly reading my palm and awakening my life.

Kay Fittes—for your mentorship, enthusiasm, and support throughout this book launch.

Dr. Helane Androne—for introducing me to the *Don't Write That Book* Podcast

Michael Dukes—for being an advanced reader and always encouraging my efforts.

Alex Tomblin—for being an advanced reader and always being honest.

Jose Mejia—for years of support, encouragement, and being a real friend since sixth grade.

Thanks

Tim Ferriss—for writing *The 4-Hour Workweek* and opening up a whole can of crazy, beautiful worms.

Tony Robbins—for teaching me the principles that changed my life from "have to" to "get to."

Brendon Burchard—for high-performance mentorship.

Dean Graziosi and the Mastermind.com team—for showing what contribution looks like in action.

Chandler Bolt, Scott Allan, and the entire team at Self-Publishing—for helping me bring this book to life.

Martin Scorsese—for showing me what mastery looks like.

Blake Snyder—for *Save the Cat*, the framework that inspired this one.

Mike Michalowicz and AJ Harper—for your leadership and education in authorship.

Special Thanks

To every client, student, and audience member who trusted me with their transformation: your courage gave me the evidence that this methodology works.

And finally, to you—the reader—for having the audacity to direct your own life in a world that profits from keeping you dull and disconnected.

Keep directing.

REFERENCES

(These works influenced the philosophy and tools in this book.)

BOOKS CITED

Bandler, R., & Grinder, J. (1975). The Structure of Magic I: A Book About Language and Therapy. Science and Behavior Books.

Burchard, B. (2017). High Performance Habits: How Extraordinary People Become That Way. Hay House.

Campbell, J. (1949). The Hero with a Thousand Faces. Pantheon Books.

Dweck, C. S. (2006). Mindset: The New Psychology of Success. Random House.

Ferriss, T. (2007). The 4-Hour Workweek: Escape 9–5, Live Anywhere, and Join the New Rich. Crown Publishers.

Fogg, B. J. (2019). Tiny Habits: The Small Changes That Change Everything. Houghton Mifflin Harcourt.

Frankl, V. E. (1946). Man's Search for Meaning. Beacon Press.

Hill, N. (1937). Think and Grow Rich. The Ralston Society.

Holiday, R. (2016). Ego Is the Enemy. Portfolio.

Mandino, O. (1968). The Greatest Salesman in the World. Frederick Fell Publishers.

Olson, J. (2013). The Slight Edge: Turning Simple Disciplines into Massive Success and Happiness. Greenleaf Book Group Press.

Pressfield, S. (2002). The War of Art: Break Through the Blocks and Win Your Inner Creative Battles. Black Irish Entertainment.

Robbins, A. (1991). Awaken the Giant Within: How to Take Immediate Control of Your Mental, Emotional, Physical and Financial Destiny. Free Press.

Robbins, T., Diamandis, P. H., & Hariri, R. (2022). Life Force. Simon & Schuster.

Snyder, B. (2005). Save the Cat!: The Last Book on Screenwriting You'll Ever Need. Michael Wiese Productions.

Vogler, C. (2007). The Writer's Journey: Mythic Structure for Writers (3rd ed.). Michael Wiese Productions.

Waitzkin, J. (2007). The Art of Learning. Free Press.

Willink, J. (2017). Discipline Equals Freedom: Field Manual. St. Martin's Press.

Csikszentmihalyi, M. (1990). Flow: The Psychology of Optimal Experience. Harper & Row.

Singer, M. A. (2007). The Untethered Soul. New Harbinger Publications.

Millman, D. (1980). Way of the Peaceful Warrior. H.J. Kramer.

Coyle, D. (2009). The Talent Code. Bantam Dell.

Dalio, R. (2017). Principles. Simon & Schuster.

Kwik, J. (2020). Limitless. Hay House.

Asprey, D. (2014). The Bulletproof Diet. Rodale.

Walker, M. (2017). Why We Sleep. Scribner.

Powers, T. J. (2023). The Dose Effect. Self-published.

PHILOSOPHICAL & HISTORICAL SOURCES

Aurelius, M. (180 CE). Meditations (G. Hays, Trans., 2002). Modern Library.

Laozi. (c. 4th century BCE). Tao Te Ching (S. Mitchell, Trans., 1988). Harper Perennial.

Dostoevsky, F. (1864). Notes from Underground. Various editions.

Jung, C. G. (1964). Man and His Symbols. Doubleday.

Plato. (399 BCE). Apology.

Campbell, J. (1991). Reflections on the Art of Living (D. K. Osbon, Ed.). HarperCollins.

RESEARCH & ACADEMIC SOURCES

Harvard Business School. (2019). Research on entrepreneurial action-taking under uncertainty. Harvard Business Review.

Little, B. R. (2014). Personality, personal projects, and free traits. Journal of Personality and Social Psychology.

LinkedIn Talent Solutions. (2023). Global Talent Trends Report.

Stanford University. Research on decision-making, life satisfaction, and cognitive performance.

University of California, Berkeley. (2019). Creativity and neural plasticity following travel and environmental change. Journal of Cognitive Neuroscience.

UCLA Center for Health Policy Research. Studies on stress, anxiety, and depression in high-density urban environments.

Ware, B. (2012). The Top Five Regrets of the Dying. Hay House.

NOTES ON ATTRIBUTION

Some quotations and ideas are widely circulated within philosophy, psychology, and personal development literature. In cases where exact origins are debated, attribution reflects the most commonly accepted source or thematic origin. All references are used for educational, transformational, and illustrative purposes under fair use principles.

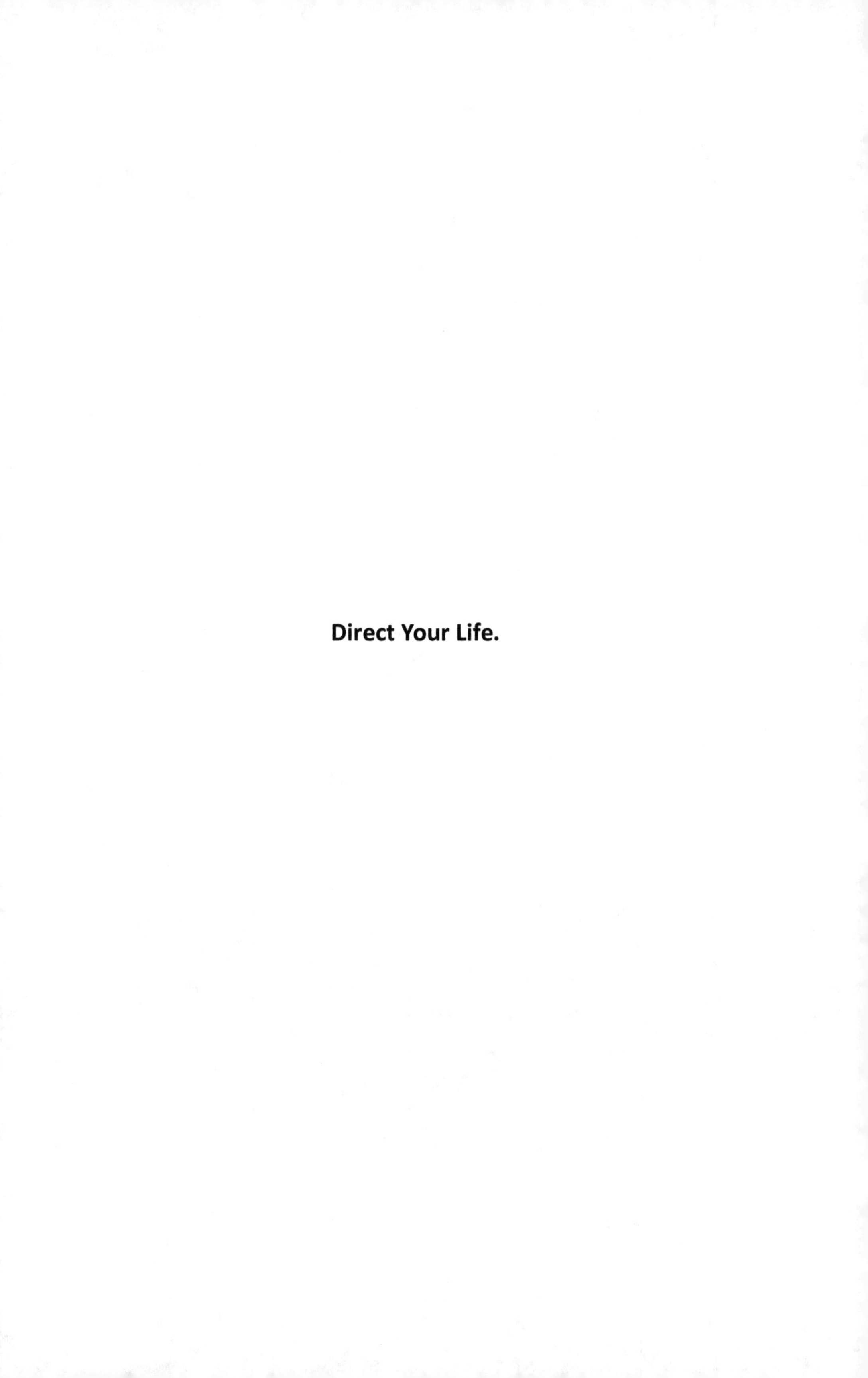

Direct Your Life.

www.ingramcontent.com/pod-product-compliance
Lightning Source LLC
Chambersburg PA
CBHW070850160726
48004CB00003B/1003